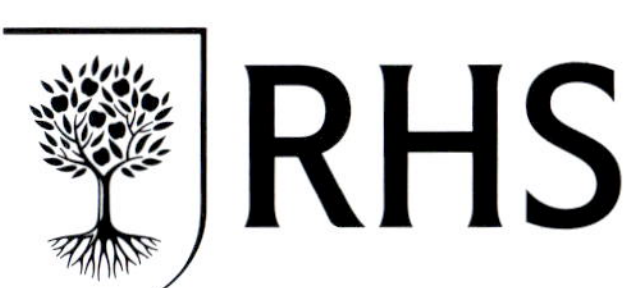

BOTANICAL ART

THE WATERCOLOUR ART PAD

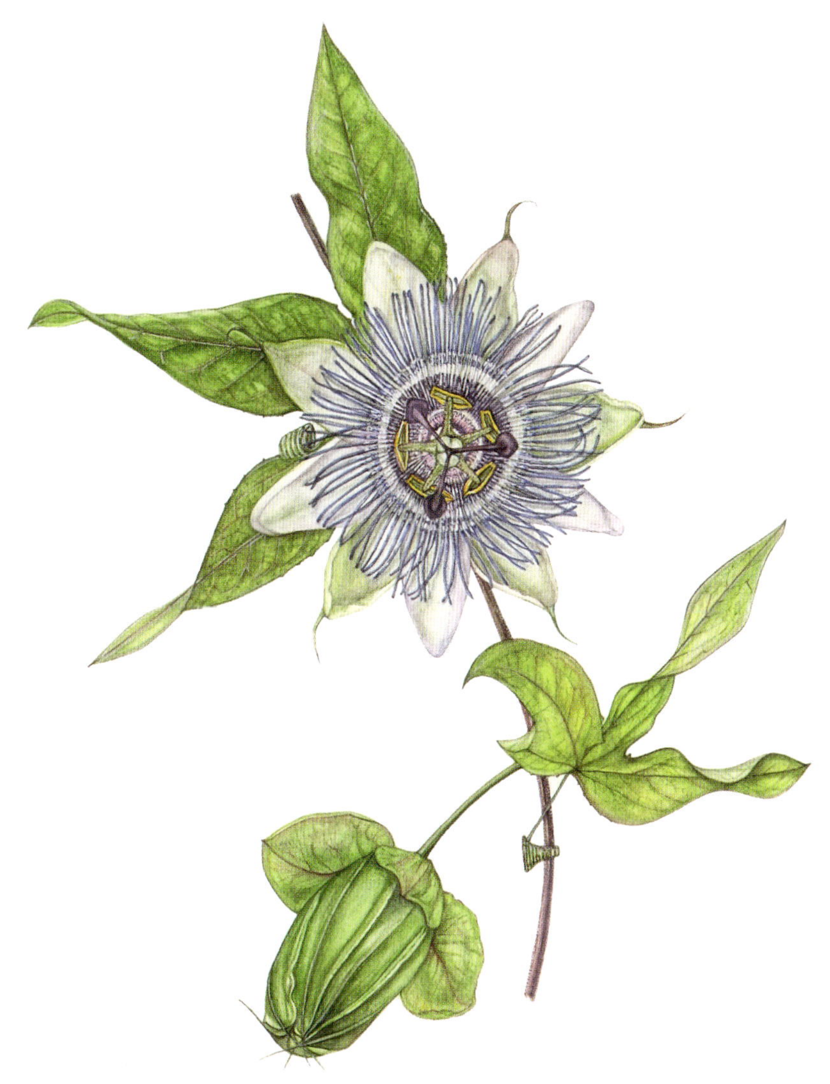

RACHEL PEDDER-SMITH

MITCHELL
BEAZLEY

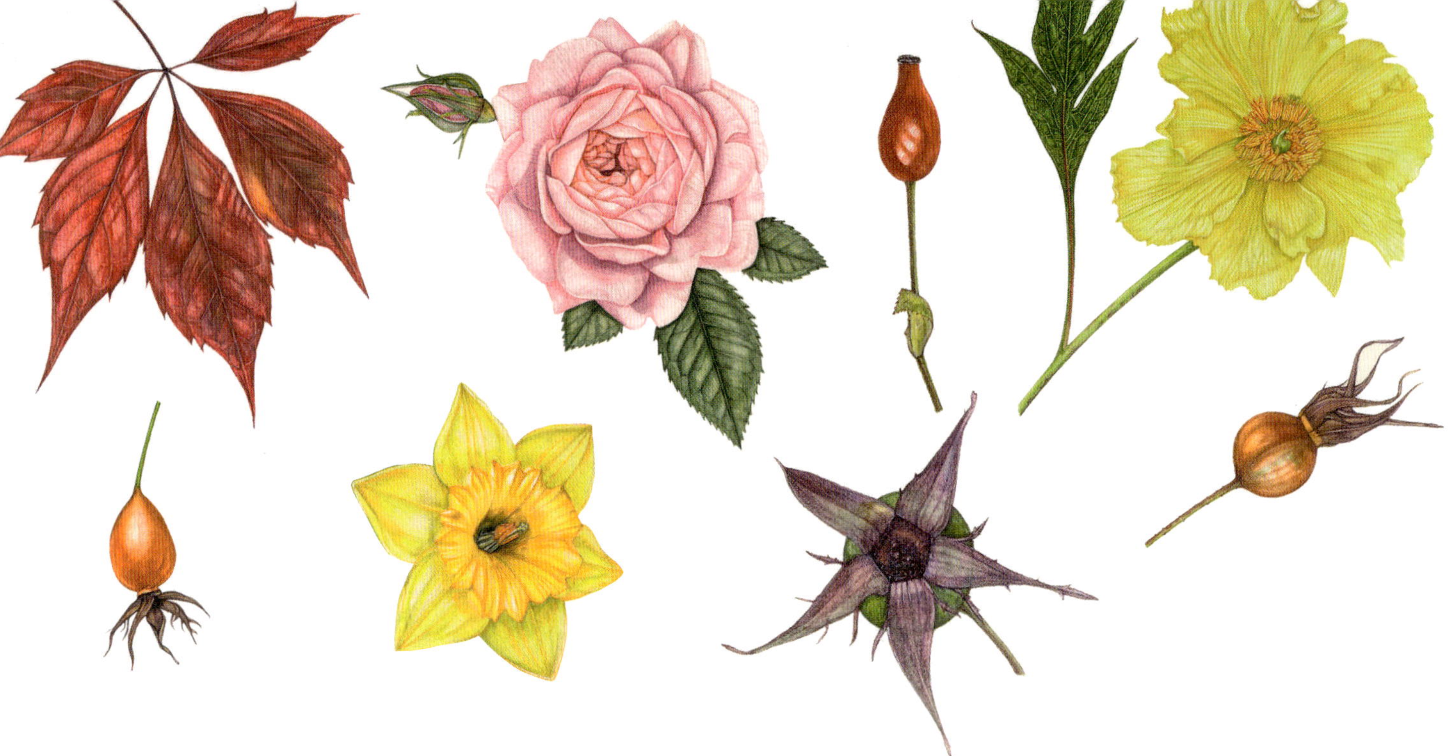

The Royal Horticultural Society is the UK's leading gardening charity dedicated to advancing horticulture and promoting good gardening. Its charitable work includes providing expert advice and information, training the next generation of gardeners, creating hands-on opportunities for children to grow plants and conducting research into plants, pests and environmental issues affecting gardeners.

For more information, visit www.rhs.org.uk or call 0845 130 4646

First published in Great Britain in 2021 by Mitchell Beazley
a division of Octopus Publishing Group Limited
Carmelite House
50 Victoria Embankment
London EC4Y 0DZ
www.octopusbooks.co.uk

An Hachette UK Company
www.hachette.co.uk

The authorized representative in the EEA is Hachette Ireland,
8 Castlecourt Centre, Dublin 15, D15 XTP3, Ireland (email: info@hbgi.ie)

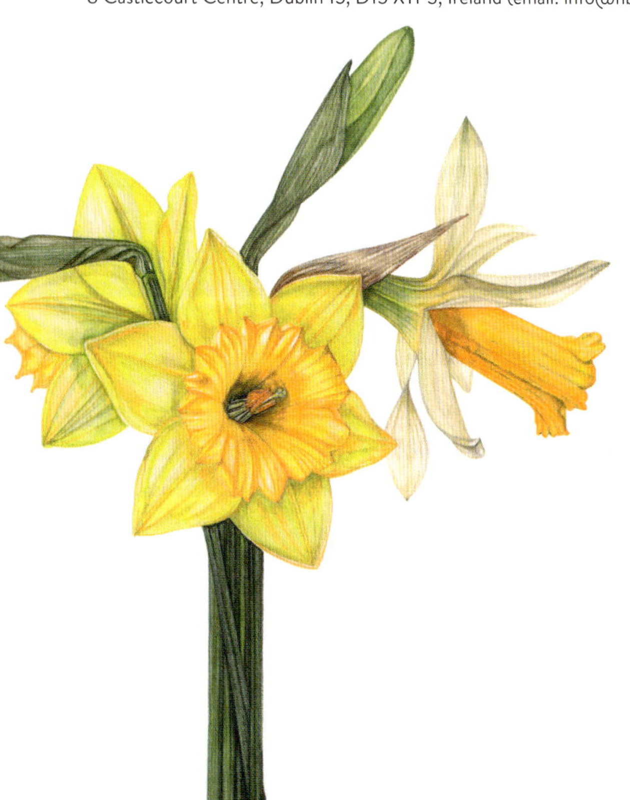

Published in association with the Royal Horticultural Society

Distributed in the US by Hachette Book Group
1290 Avenue of the Americas
4th and 5th Floors
New York, NY 10104

Distributed in Canada by Canadian Manda Group
664 Annette St.
Toronto
Ontario
Canada M6S 2C8

A CIP record for this book is available from the British Library

ISBN 978-1-78472-806-9

This book was conceived, designed and produced by
The Bright Press, an imprint of the Quarto Group
1 Triptych Place, London, SE1 9SH, United Kingdom

Designer: www.wheeldesign.co.uk
Project Editor: Emily Angus
Publisher: James Evans
Mitchell Beazley Publisher: Alison Starling
RHS Publisher: Helen Griffin

All illustrations by Rachel Pedder-Smith

10 9 8 7

Printed in Huizhou, Guangdong, China
TT/03/26

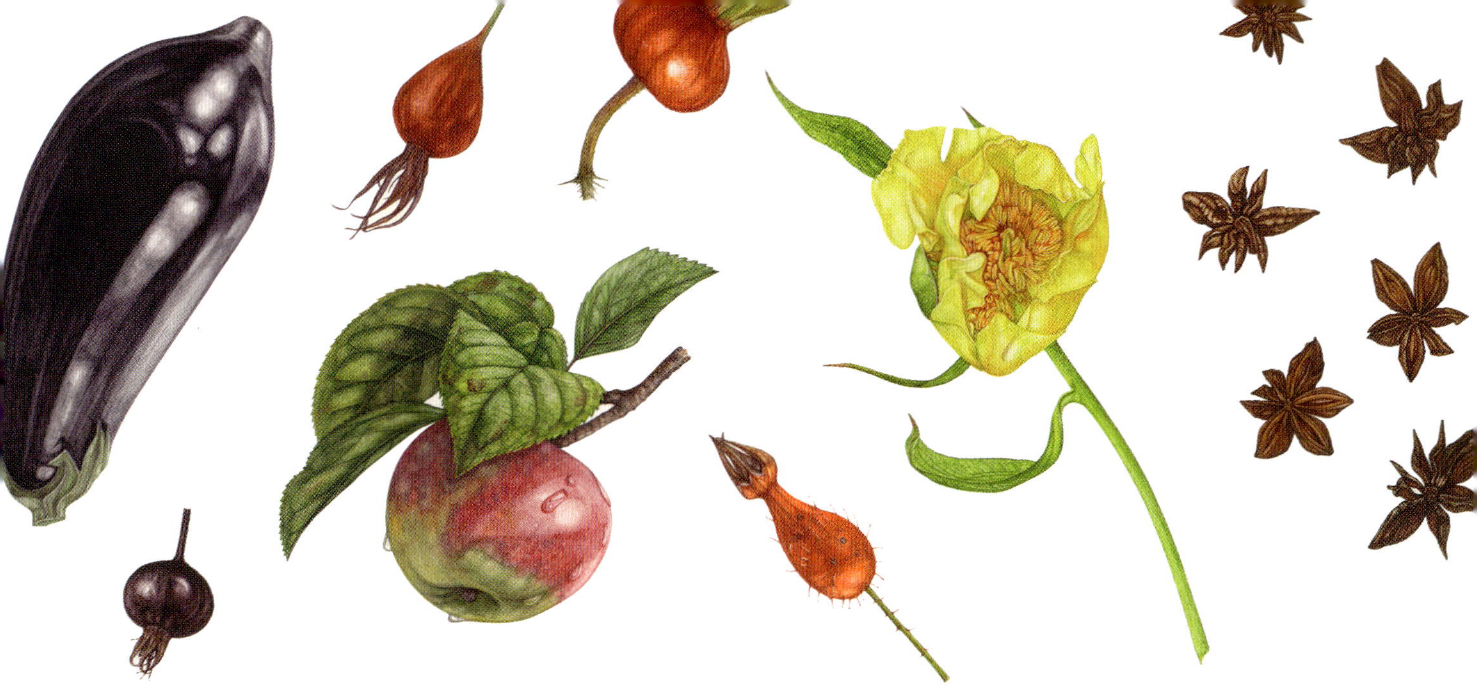

CONTENTS

Get Painting

Turn to the art paper at page 25 and pull out a page to get started.

Introduction

My favourite moment in painting is when the object has been drawn out and I use the wet-on-wet technique (see page 7) to make my first mark. Using clean water, I wet the area I want to colour, mix my first colour wash, drop it onto the damp paper and watch how – as if by magic – the paint spreads to the outer limit of the damp area. This is a captivating moment every time – the first step to a new piece of art.

Watercolour has been the traditional medium used for botanical art for a number of reasons. In previous centuries, on voyages of discovery when ships' artists needed to record the exotic plants they saw, they favoured watercolour for its versatility, subtlety, portability and ability to capture the delicate and sometimes ethereal nature of petals. The same is true today, and watercolours are easy to use wherever you are – from your studio or kitchen table to in the field.

To produce good watercolour pieces you do not have to have a massive range of paints; I have a medium-sized travel paint box and regularly use just 25 different colours. I use pans rather than tubes as I find these really accessible and quick to use, but there is no real difference in the end results. It is really important to use professional quality paints as they have more pigment and are not chalky, unlike student quality watercolours. I use the metal leaves of my paint travel set as a palette and I never wash the colours off, as they often come in very useful on another day! When I get short of space I clean off a small section with a tissue.

There are 15 paintings to produce in this book with a full range of textures and weights, from the light and sensitive petals of a rose or daffodil, to the shining depth and darkness of an aubergine skin. I hope you enjoy painting them.

Rachel Pedder-Smith

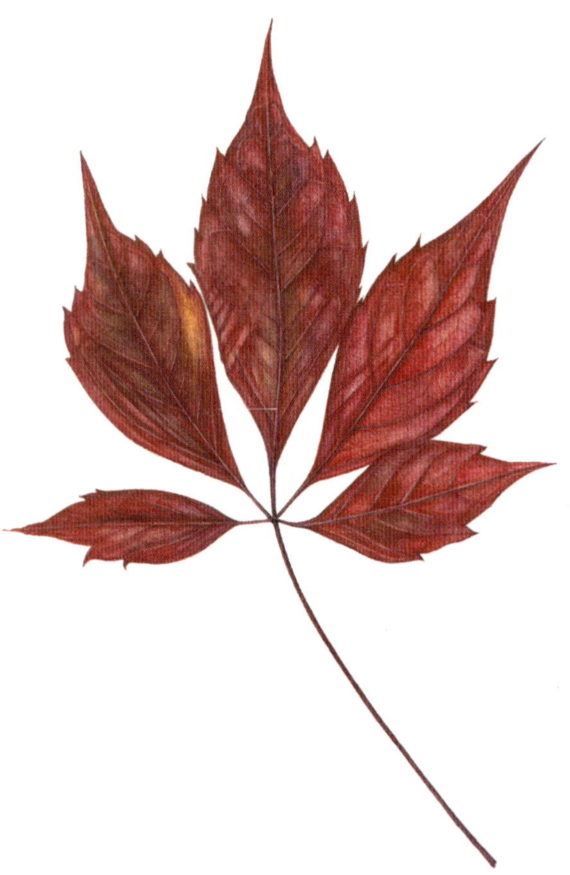

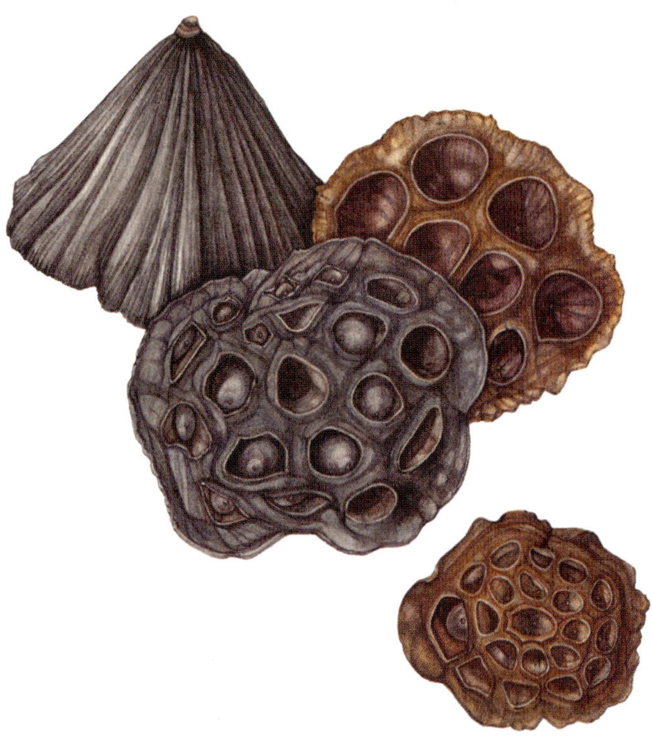

How to use this book

Select a subject

Choose the object you want to paint from the outlines printed on the art paper at the back of the book.

Pull out the sheet

Remove the sheet by pressing down on the opposite page and pulling firmly but carefully. Secure it to a surface by taping it down with masking tape along all four edges. This will help to prevent the paper buckling when wet.

Refer to the Gallery

As you paint, refer to the original artwork and the recommended colour palettes in the gallery on pages 16–24. Each colour used in this book has been given a number – see the complete palette on page 6.

Advice for beginners

For guidance on how to get started with watercolours, turn to page 6. As well as describing the equipment you'll need, it shows the full palette of colours used in this book, with their names and key numbers. Before you embark on your first project, using spare paper, practise the watercolour techniques described on page 7 and try the tutorials on the pages that follow.

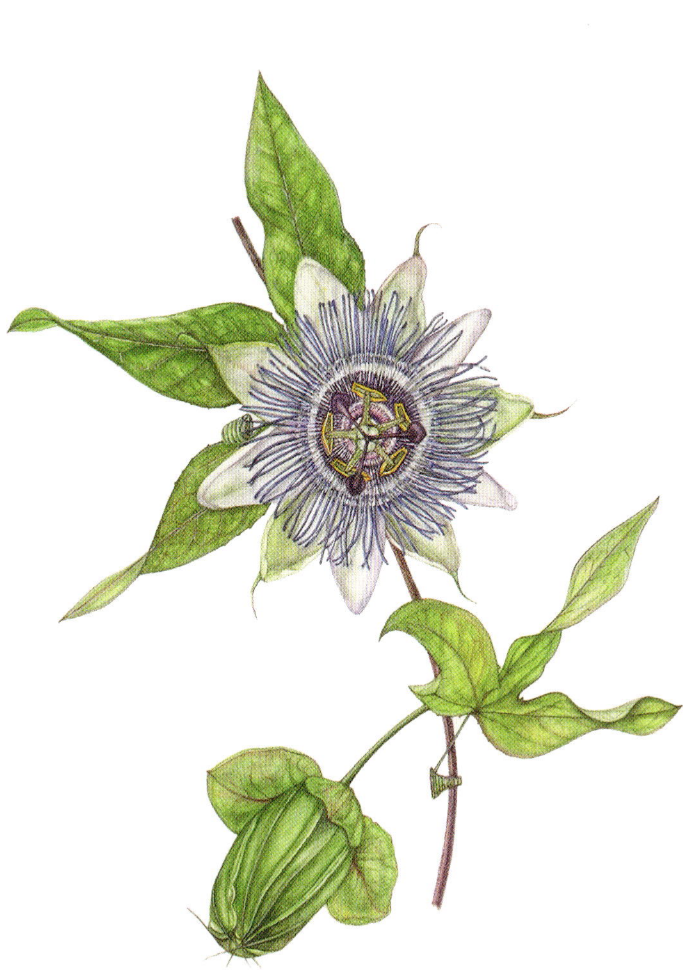

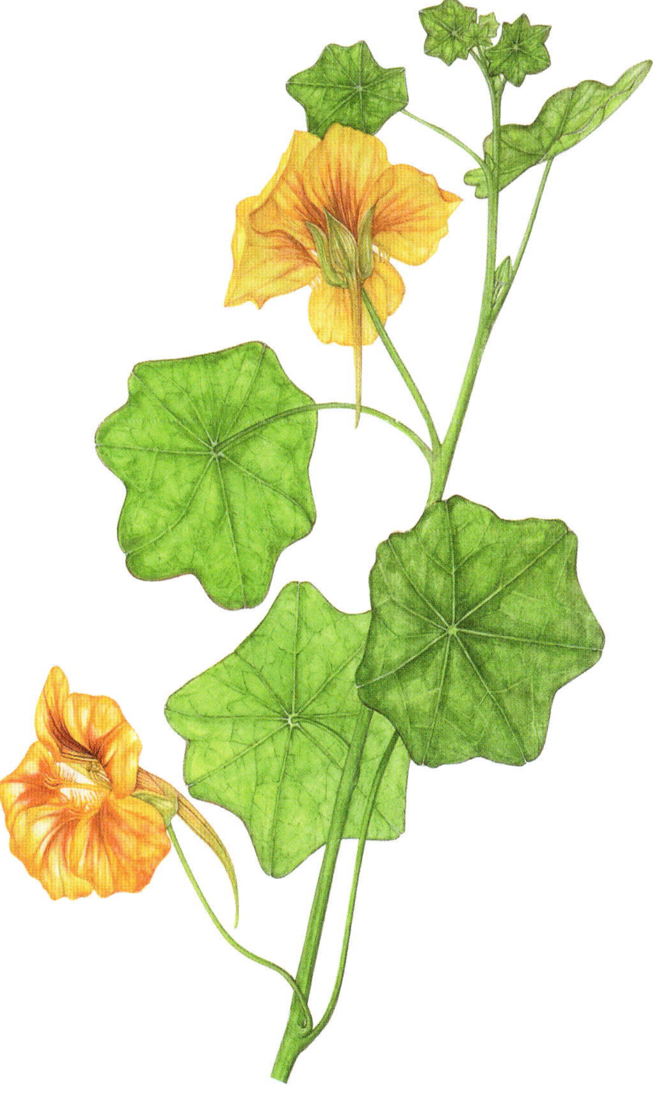

Getting started

Flower painter's toolkit

Before you embark on your adventure as a watercolour flower painter, you'll need to have some basic kit. Listed here are the essential tools and materials you'll need to recreate the botanical paintings in this book.

Paints

For rich, jewel-like colour, it's really important to use professional-quality paints, as these contain more pigment. You can buy them in tubes or pans (little blocks); pans have the advantage of being really easy and quick to work with. The paintings in this book require 24 different colours – you can see them listed on the right. In some cases you may have to combine many colours to create the right one for a particular petal.

Palette

The metal leaves of a travel paint set make a very handy palette, and it's a good idea never to wash the colours off – they often come in very useful on another day. If you start to run short of space, just clean off a small section with a tissue. If you don't have a purpose-made palette, you could use a white ceramic plate instead.

Brushes

You'll need four sizes of paintbrush: a size 6, a size 4, a size 000 and a size 0000. These are a synthetic and sable mix and keep their fine point for longer than pure sable; they are also more reasonably priced. The largest brush is ideal for the initial washes and the smaller brushes can be used for all of the detail, reserving the size 0000 for fine lines.

Paper towels

It is essential to have a tissue or paper towels to hand as you paint. You'll find you use them frequently, whether to wipe colour off the brush when using a dry-brush technique, to create highlights by lifting colour off the paper, or to remove colour immediately if you make a mistake.

Masking fluid

This can be useful for masking out small, precise areas that you want to retain as highlights. It comes in bottles or in a handy pen form that allows you to apply the fluid directly via the nib. If applying with a brush, dip the brush into a detergent solution first and wipe off the excess moisture with paper towels before dipping it into the fluid, to prevent clogging. Allow the fluid to dry completely before painting over it.

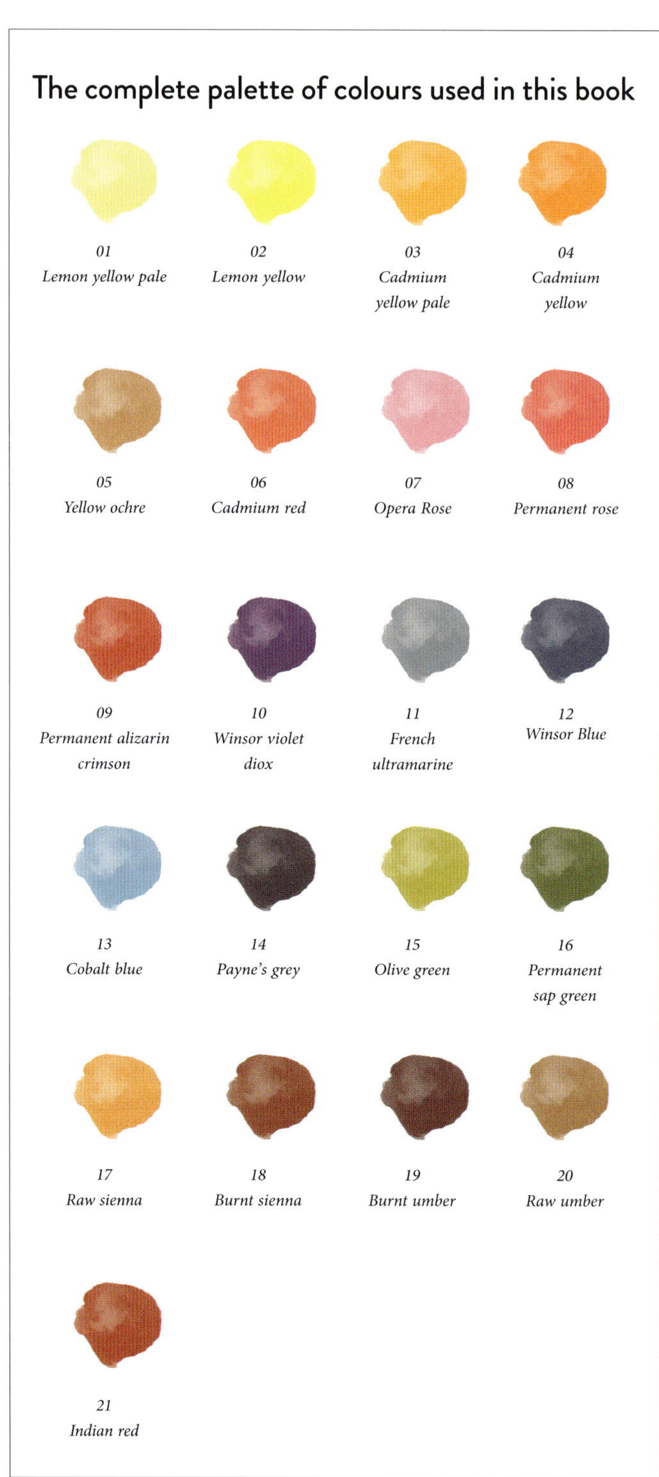

The complete palette of colours used in this book

Watercolour terms and techniques

There are a few key watercolour techniques that you'll use again and again on the different projects in this book. Try them out on spare paper first so that you really get to know how to use them.

Making a wash

Watercolour paint needs to be mixed with water to liquefy it. The more water you add, the thinner the mixture will be and the lighter the colour. This combination of paint and water is known as a 'wash'. Dip your brush into water and then load it with your desired colour. Use your palette to adjust the balance of colour to water or to mix with other colours.

Painting wet-on-wet

The wet-on-wet technique involves painting onto wet paper or paint. Use this technique only when applying the first wash. First, wet the paper using a large brush and clean water. Take it only as far as you want the colour to spread and leave highlighted areas dry. Now apply the first wash of colour with a large brush and watch the paint flow evenly over the wet surface to the edge, where it will stop, leaving a distinct line or watermark. You can add in different colours while still wet.

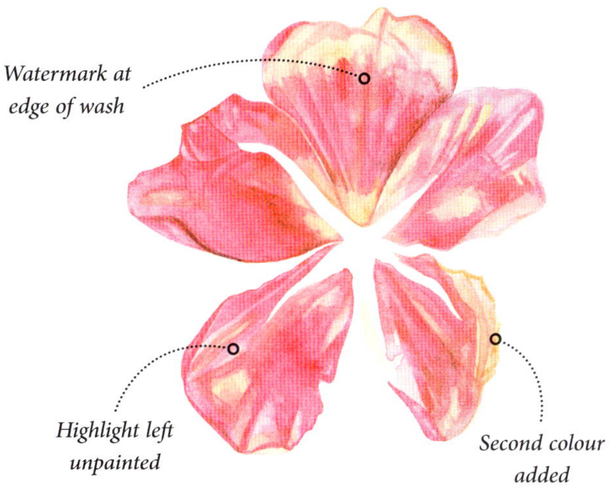

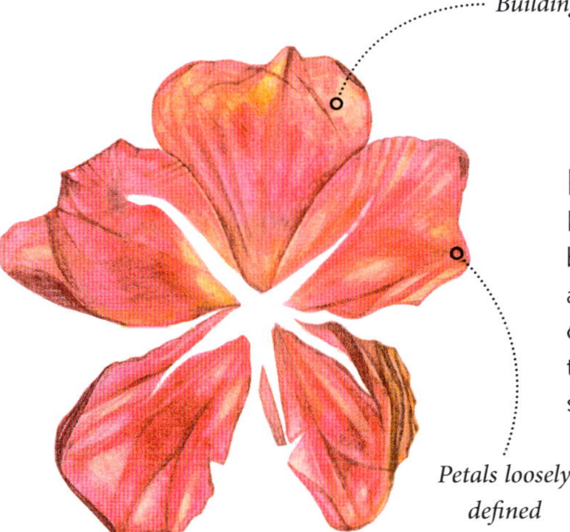

Painting wet-on-dry

For this technique, you wait for the previous layer of paint to dry before applying the next. Use this method to build up the colour after applying the first wash. Working on a dry surface gives greater control over the spread of the paint. Use a large brush to apply the wash to the dry paper in certain areas, building up the colour, shading and giving loose definition to the petals.

Using a dry-brush

This method allows you to add fine detail to your painting with a small brush – using the brush almost like a pencil. Dip the brush into the paint regularly but wipe it carefully on some paper towels to remove any excess colour before touching the paper. Use the dry-brush technique to build up texture with fine lines and tiny vein details.

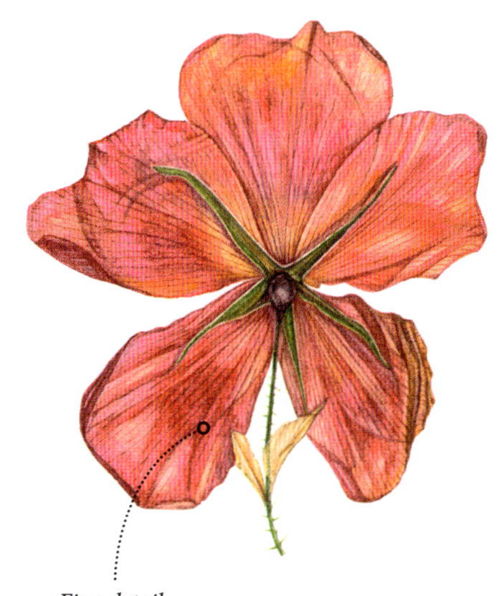

How to paint a group of flowers

Daffodils make great subject matters to paint as they look so different from every angle and are such sculptural forms. When painting yellows, use clean water and try to keep the light areas really clear and bright.

1. Mix cadmium yellow pale, lemon yellow and permanent sap green and apply to the petals followed by cadmium yellow pale on the trumpet, leaving the lightest areas white on both. Next use a lemon yellow wash over the whole flower, keeping a few white areas of the petals clear.

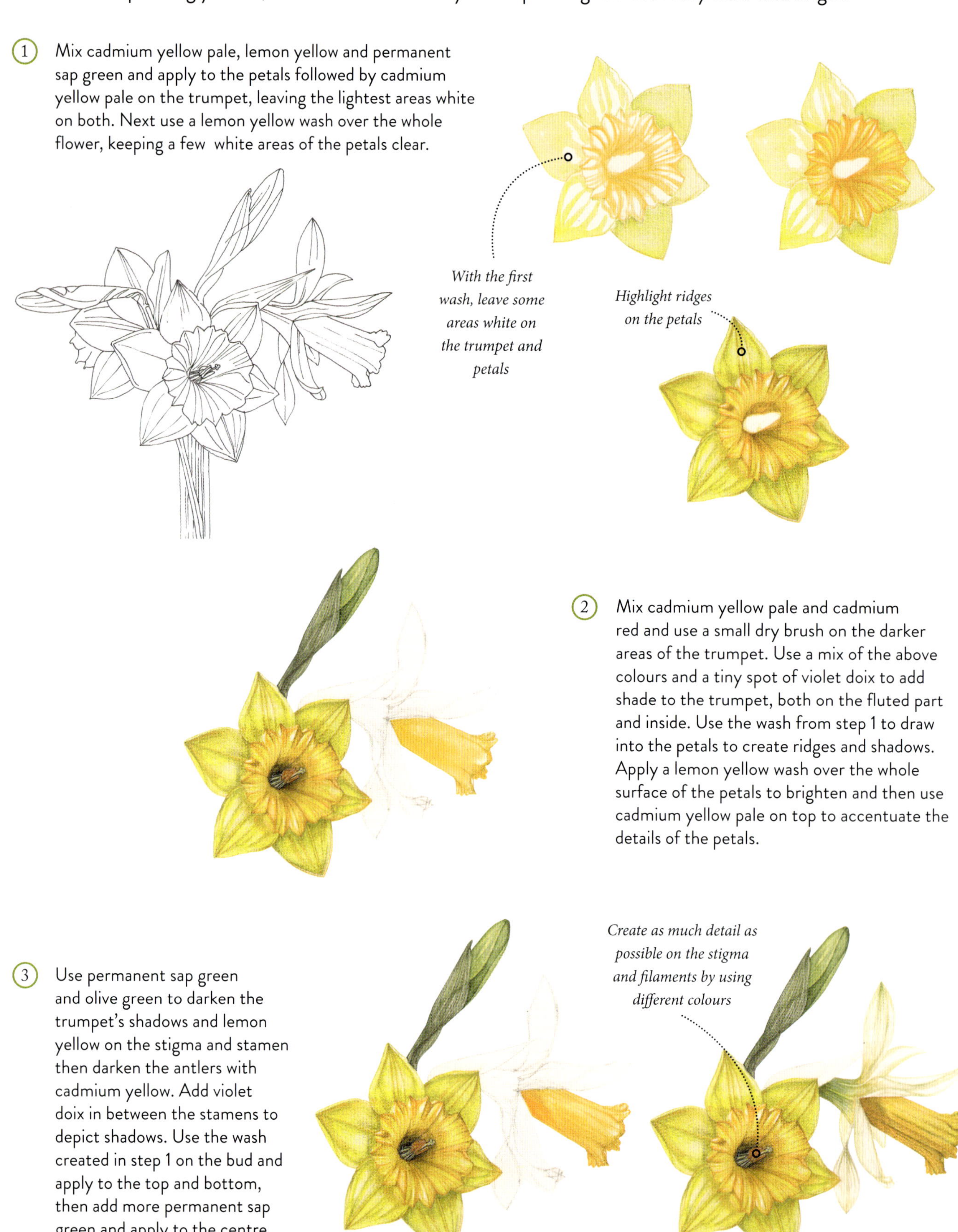

2. Mix cadmium yellow pale and cadmium red and use a small dry brush on the darker areas of the trumpet. Use a mix of the above colours and a tiny spot of violet doix to add shade to the trumpet, both on the fluted part and inside. Use the wash from step 1 to draw into the petals to create ridges and shadows. Apply a lemon yellow wash over the whole surface of the petals to brighten and then use cadmium yellow pale on top to accentuate the details of the petals.

3. Use permanent sap green and olive green to darken the trumpet's shadows and lemon yellow on the stigma and stamen then darken the antlers with cadmium yellow. Add violet doix in between the stamens to depict shadows. Use the wash created in step 1 on the bud and apply to the top and bottom, then add more permanent sap green and apply to the centre.

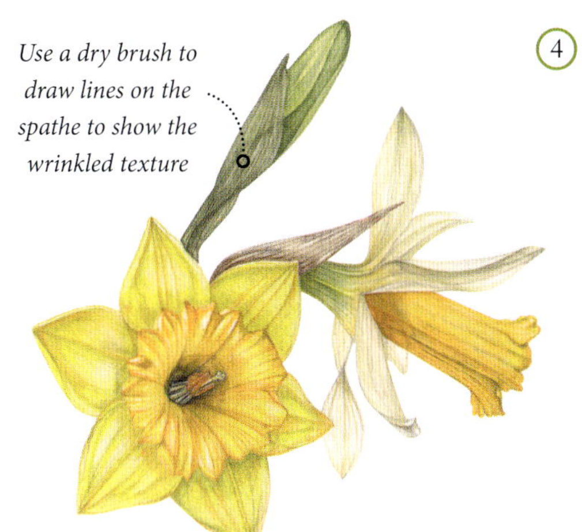

(4) Mix permanent sap green, olive green and burnt umber and paint this wash over the spathe (the papery sleeve covering the bud). Then use the dark green wash to show dark areas on the petals of the bud, especially where the petals overlap each other. Paint the trumpet on the next open flower all over with a cadmium yellow pale wash.

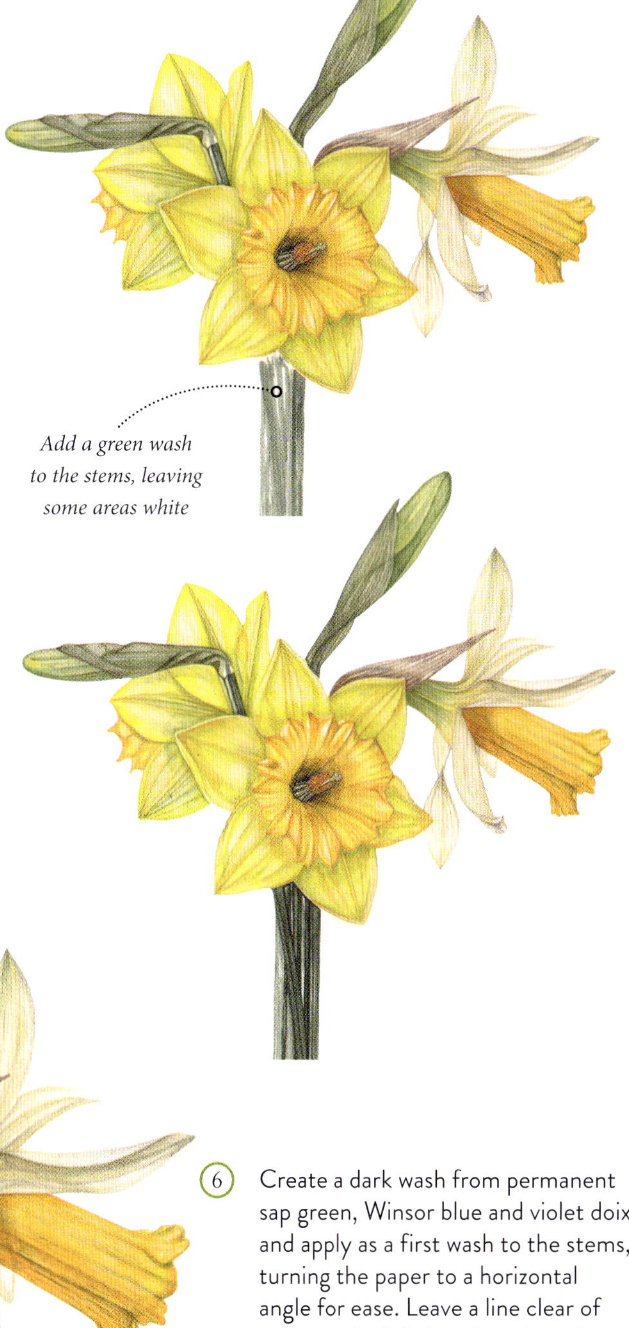

(5) Mix cadmium pale yellow and cadmium red to add detail to the trumpet and a cadmium pale yellow to the base of the petals. Add a tiny bit of violet doix to this wash to add shadows behind the trumpet. Use a permanent sap green wash on a dry brush on the base of the petals to draw in the markings. Using lots of water, mix lemon yellow, cadmium yellow pale and permanent sap green and apply to the petals, leaving some areas white. Mix permanent sap green and violet doix to create shadows, then use a small, dry brush to apply a violet doix and cadmium yellow pale wash for the lines of the white petals. Next, add a light permanent sap green line down the back of the reversed petals.

(6) Create a dark wash from permanent sap green, Winsor blue and violet doix and apply as a first wash to the stems, turning the paper to a horizontal angle for ease. Leave a line clear of paint on the left-hand section of each stem. Next use a dry-brush technique to draw with the paint and highlight the twists in the stems. As a final touch, apply a light lemon yellow wash over the whole of the stems to brighten them up.

How to paint shiny surfaces

An aubergine is the perfect example for this tutorial on painting dark and shiny surfaces as it has a wonderfully rich and complex colour that watercolour can replicate very well. This painting task is simple in its use of just two main colours and uses quite a dark first wash, but you need to be really careful to preserve the light patches and approach them carefully.

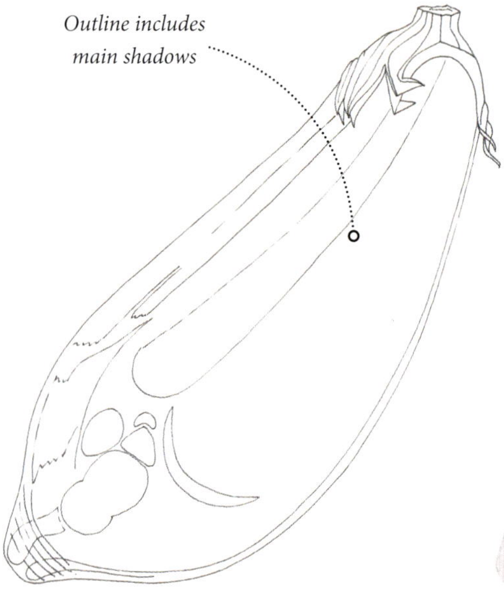

Outline includes main shadows

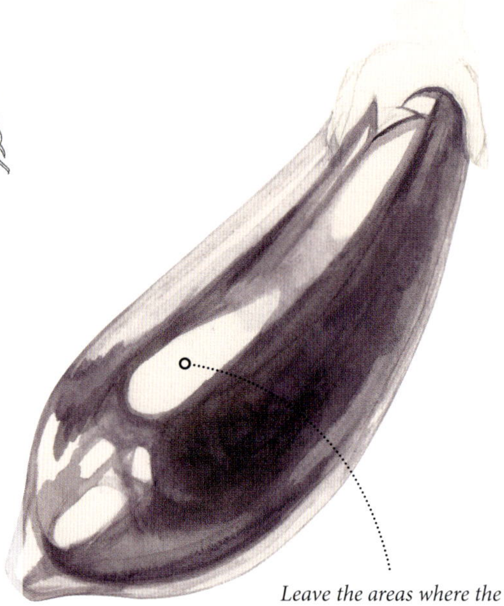

1. Mix violet doix, Payne's grey, burnt sienna and burnt umber to make the first wash. It is important to keep to the form of the aubergine using a large brush right from this first wash. Leave light areas completely white.

Leave the areas where the light hits completely white

2. Use the same colour for the second wash, adding layers to make some areas darker. Again, follow the form of the aubergine using sweeping movements with a large brush. With the third wash repeat the process of the second wash – use the same colour and carry on shading the darkest areas.

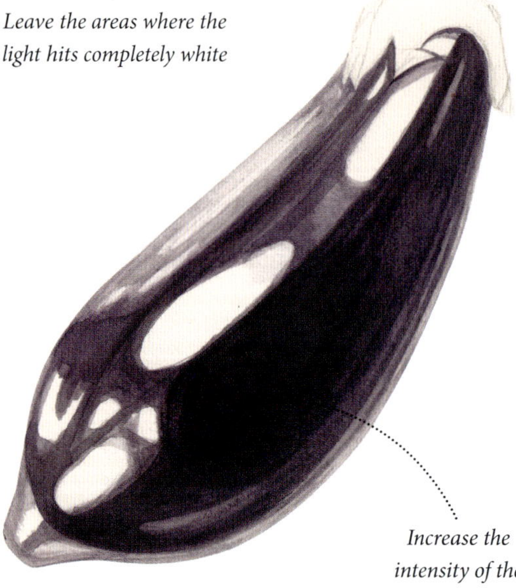

Increase the intensity of the shadows by adding more layers

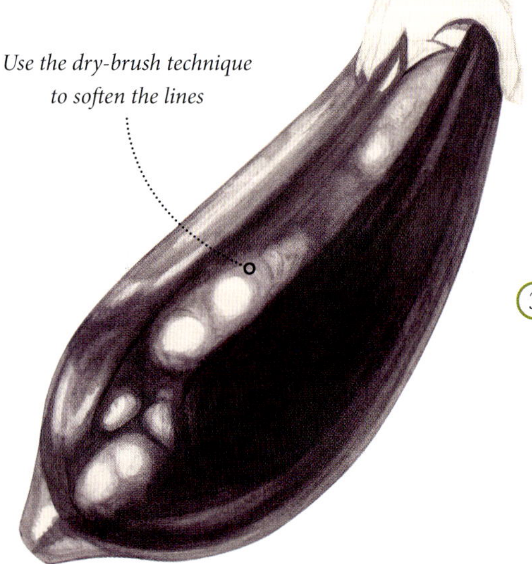

3. Change to a smaller brush, using the same dark wash mix, to define areas, focussing particularly on the sides. If you have very sharp lines from where the dark patches join up to the light areas, gently soften the edges with a large, clean brush. You may need to wet the colour and gently pad off some paint with a tissue. Then use a small brush and the dry-brush technique (see page 7) to make the edges of the light areas more hazy using tiny small lines.

4 To give the impression of texture, add a very light Payne's grey wash to some of the light patches, leaving some white patches clear. Use the first dark wash again to deepen the very dark patches, but keep some highlights running along the bottom side of the aubergine. Add some shadows in this dark wash under the calyx (green hat) at the top. Mix permanent sap green and cadmium yellow pale and use as a first wash on the calyx, leaving light areas bare.

Start filling in the highlights with light grey

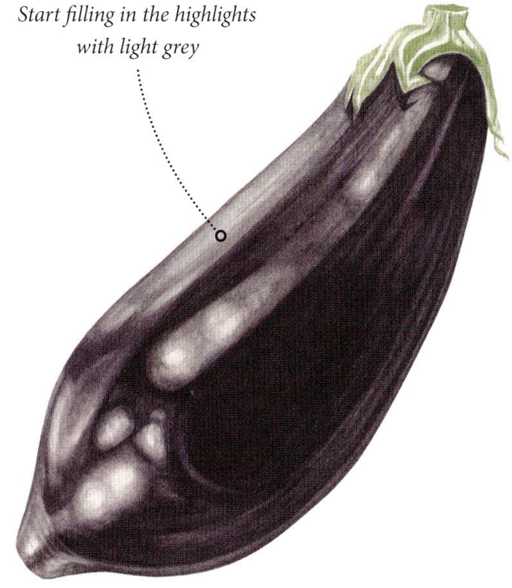

Small white lines will give the calyx texture

5 Add a second wash on the calyx in the darker sections. Mix a tiny amount of burnt umber into the calyx wash and add this to some patches to achieve a 'dirty' look. Use the main purple wash to add shadows, give the calyx form and to make it look like it wraps around the fruit. Finally, use a tiny brush and very thick paint to draw in small white lines to show white prickles on the calyx.

Layering adds definition

Steps 1 and 2 are where the bulk of the paint is applied to this design. The further steps add and define the dark patches and soften the hazy light areas.

How to paint vein details on leaves

The veins on the leaf of a plant are incredibly fine and can be tricky to capture. When painting leaves, it is important to pay attention to how the veins change from thicker, rounded skeleton-like elements that support the leaf's structure into fine life-giving veins that carry nutrients and branch out across the leaf. This tutorial is easy to follow from life as fallen leaves are very easy to come by.

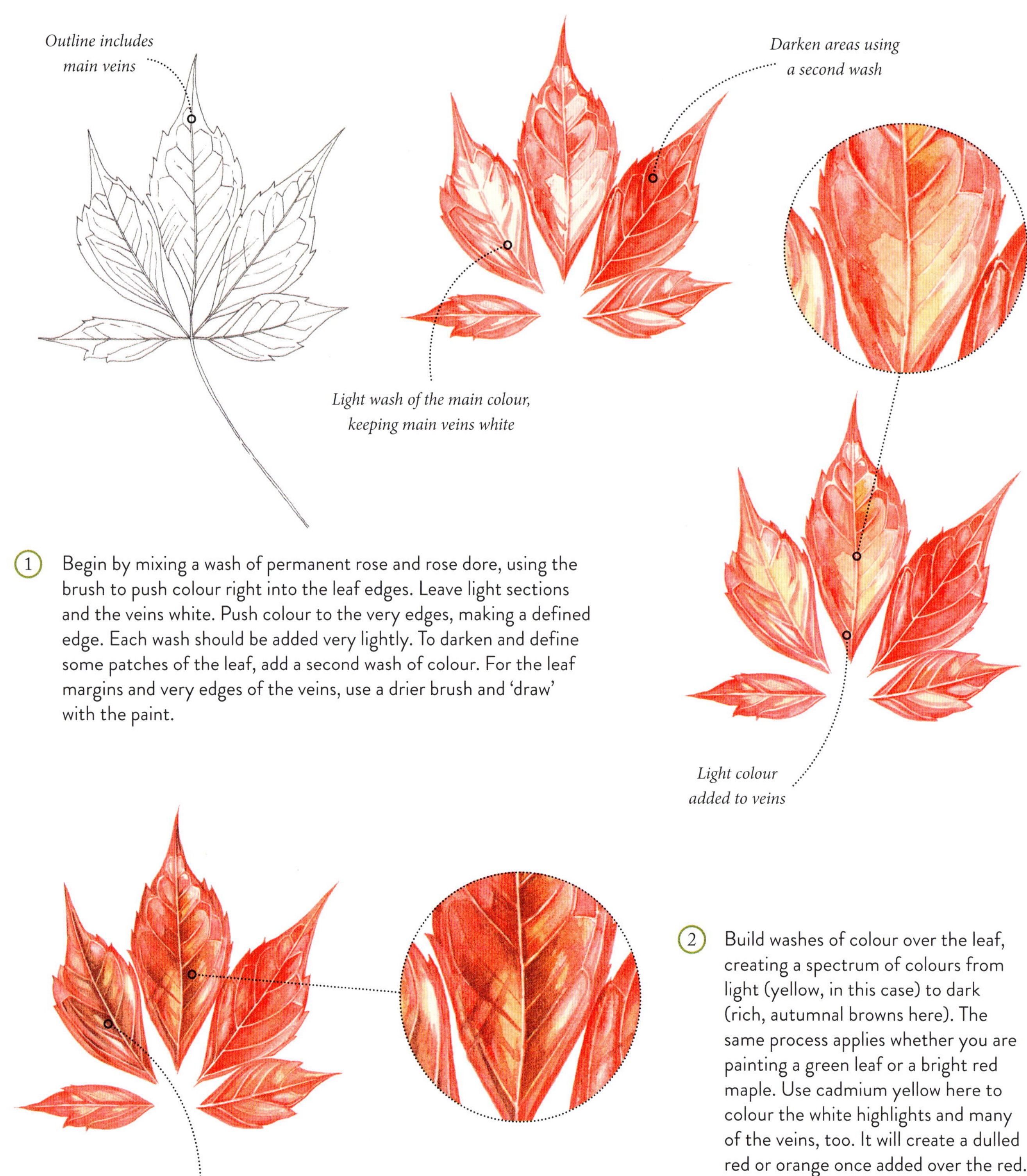

1. Begin by mixing a wash of permanent rose and rose dore, using the brush to push colour right into the leaf edges. Leave light sections and the veins white. Push colour to the very edges, making a defined edge. Each wash should be added very lightly. To darken and define some patches of the leaf, add a second wash of colour. For the leaf margins and very edges of the veins, use a drier brush and 'draw' with the paint.

2. Build washes of colour over the leaf, creating a spectrum of colours from light (yellow, in this case) to dark (rich, autumnal browns here). The same process applies whether you are painting a green leaf or a bright red maple. Use cadmium yellow here to colour the white highlights and many of the veins, too. It will create a dulled red or orange once added over the red. To strengthen colour in some areas, use a new wash of the main colour - in this case, the rich brown.

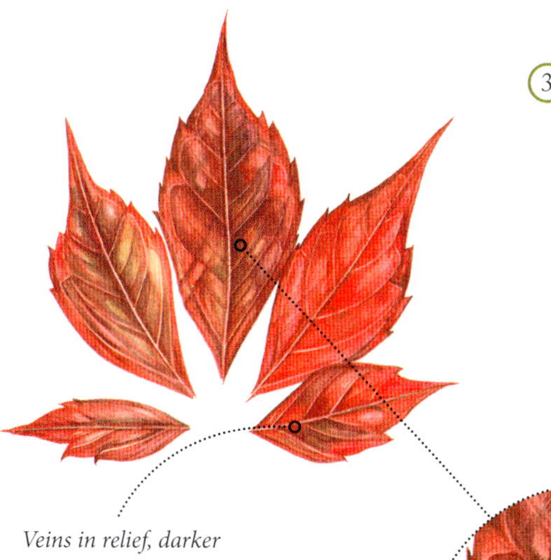

(3) With the basic leaf mapped out, you can begin to focus on adding detail around the veins using darker colours. Mix a darker wash of cadmium red, permanent alizarin crimson and violet doix and add this to the central sections that surround each major vein. To blend, add another light wash of the first red over the top. As you continue adding darker areas, reduce the size of the veins, making sure that the widest part is at the bottom of the leaf. With care, colour some areas of vein so they don't stand out too much.

Veins in relief, darker wash on one side

Create fine outlines on the very edge of major veins

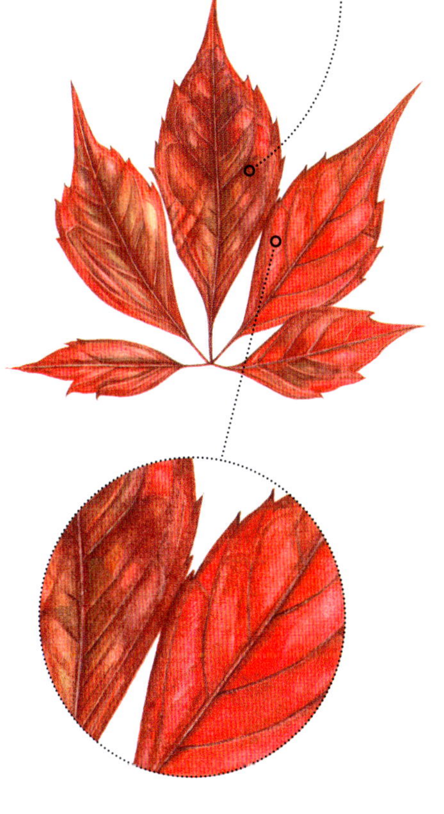

(4) Add the final washes of a new colour for realism – olive green is used here. Mix permanent alizarin crimson and violet doix and wash down one edge of the veins to create a darker, shaded side and a three-dimensional feel. Use clean water to smooth out any harsh lines. Add the small stems with a medium-dark wash, a fine brush and smooth strokes, ensuring the edges have clean, straight lines. Finally, add the main stem to complete the leaf.

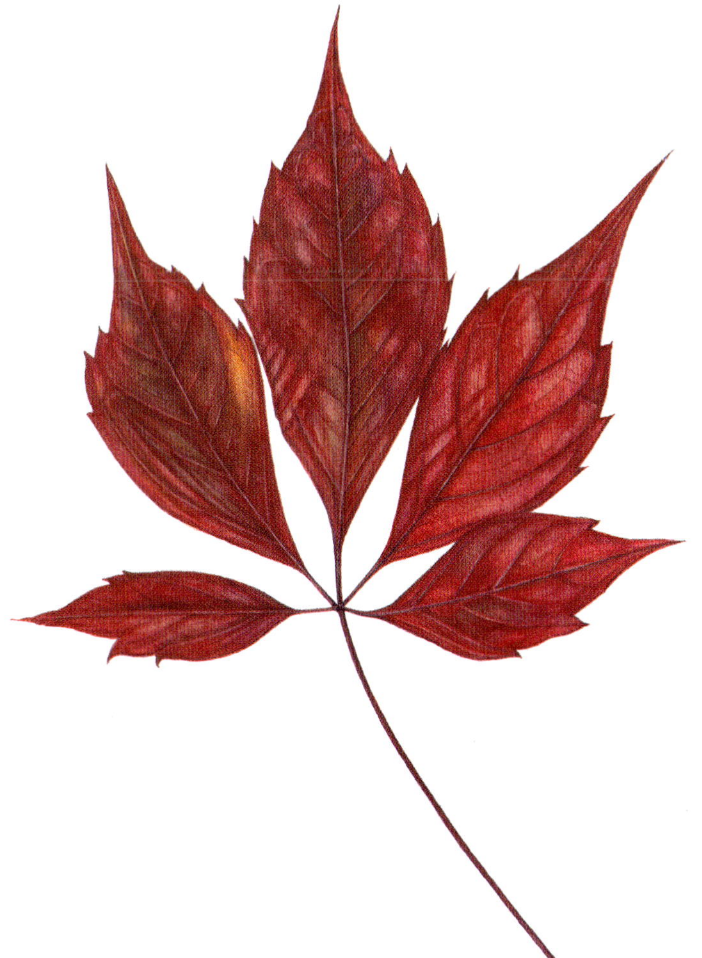

Fine details come from patient work

It is important to understand that a watercolour painting happens in small, incremental stages. Dark colours are not created by using more paint all in one go, but instead several very light washes of colour are added on top of each other to create a depth of colour. Each layer must be allowed to dry, so you need to be patient. A dry brush can be used to create finer details on top.

How to paint petals in bright light

I have chosen a rose for this tutorial as the petals are wide, often one colour and are layered next to each other so there is a lovely contrast of bright petal and cast shadow created by the bright sunlight.

1. Mix permanent rose and permanent alizarin crimson together in a very light wash, applying it to the darkest part of the petals at the centre of the rose, then move the wash outwards while it is still wet, to dissipate any harsh lines. This first wash takes some time – work on one petal at a time, looking carefully at which areas are darkest and which are so light that they need no paint whatsoever.

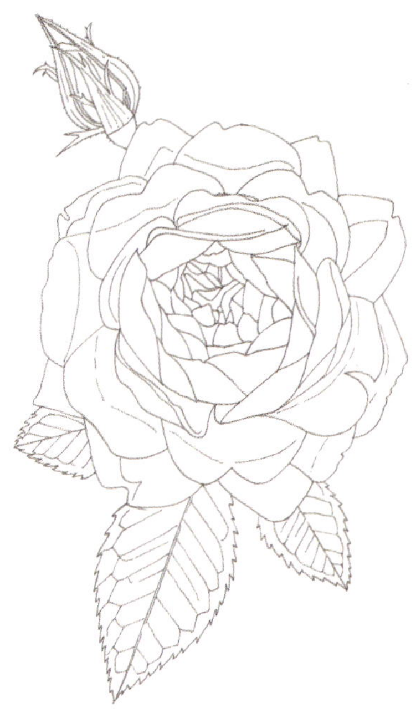

Use a light wash right from the beginning

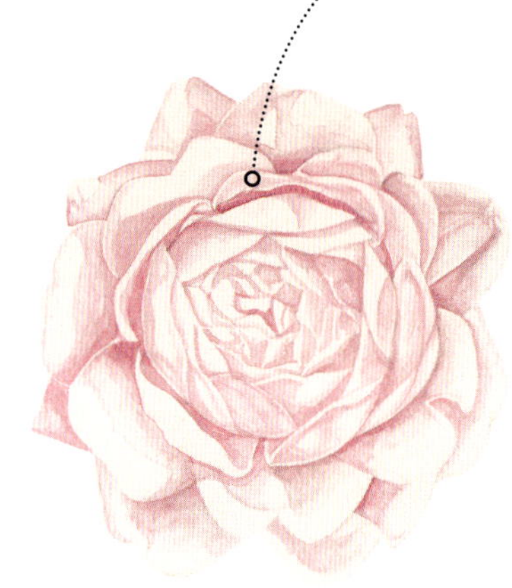

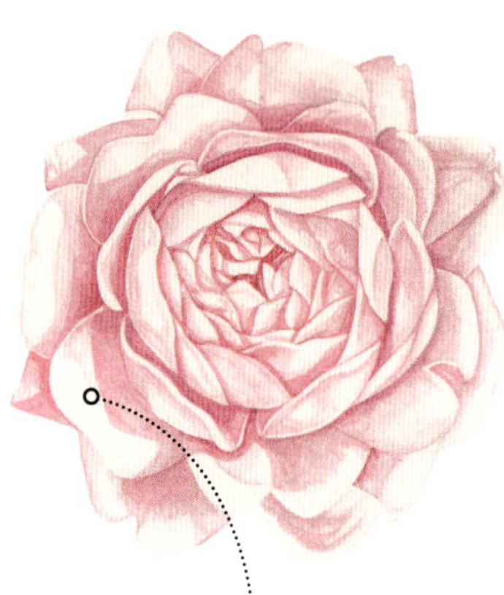

Keep some areas of the petals completely white

2. Use the same colour mix for the second wash to deepen the darkest areas, focussing on the centre part of the rose. Add a touch of violet doix into the first wash colour, and apply this to the areas where shadows are cast from one petal to another. Make sure you continue to leave the white areas white.

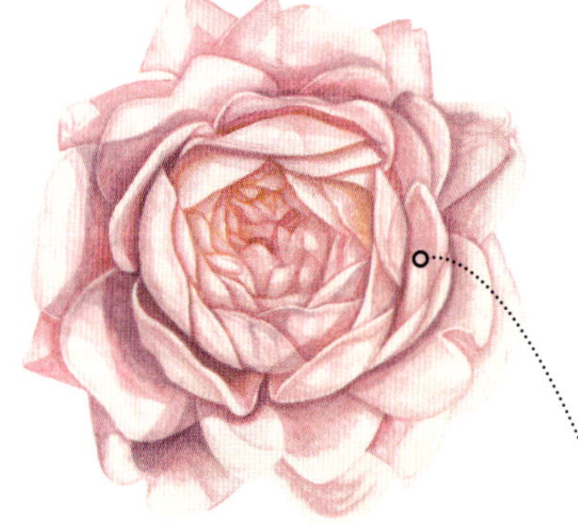

Apply darker colour to cast shadows

Use fine lines to 'draw' detail on the petals

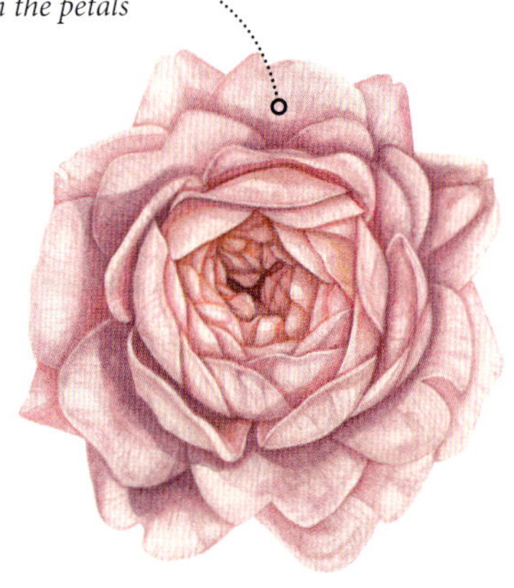

3. Mix opera rose and lemon yellow together to add a splash of bright colour to some of the darker areas, and then use it to mark out the tiny petals in the centre of the rose. Use a large, wet brush to blend out harsh lines. Add highlights to the centre petals and the pink areas by mixing cadmium red and opera rose. Apply the darker wash to show further shadows behind the petals. Go over some of the lines on the petals and the centre to make them darker.

4 For the bud, mix a wash of opera rose, permanent alizarin crimson and permanent rose. Apply this to the petals in the centre of the bud as a first wash. Reapply this wash to show darker areas of the petals. Use permanent sap green on the sepals (green parts) of the bud as the first wash. Use this same wash on the leaves – apply to the dark areas first and leave some sections white.

Still keep some areas white for highlights

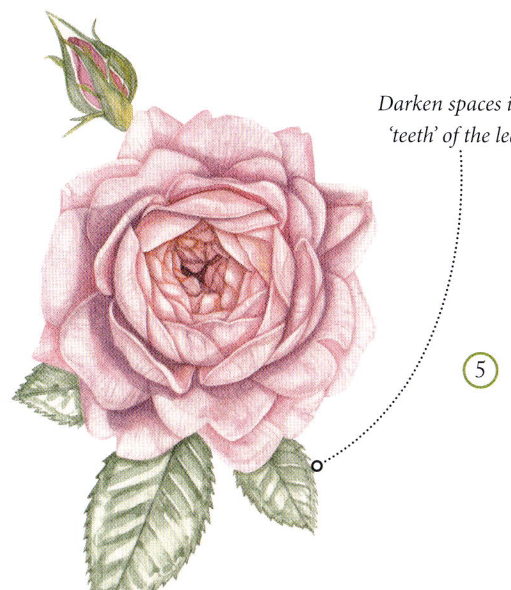

5 Mix a wash of cadmium yellow pale and permanent sap green and apply to the sepals and as a second wash on the teeth of the leaves, then use a wash of permanent sap green and olive green on the darkest areas. Add a few touches of light lemon yellow wash to the leaves and use a fine brush loaded with a dark green to add further details to the leaves and sepals. Finally use violet doix for the shadows on the white strips where the sepals touch the pink of the petals on the bud.

6 The painting could now be considered complete, but it is often good to look at this stage and then go over any details if needed. You could use a permanent rose wash to darken some lines in the petals or accentuate some of the shadows at the base of the petals.

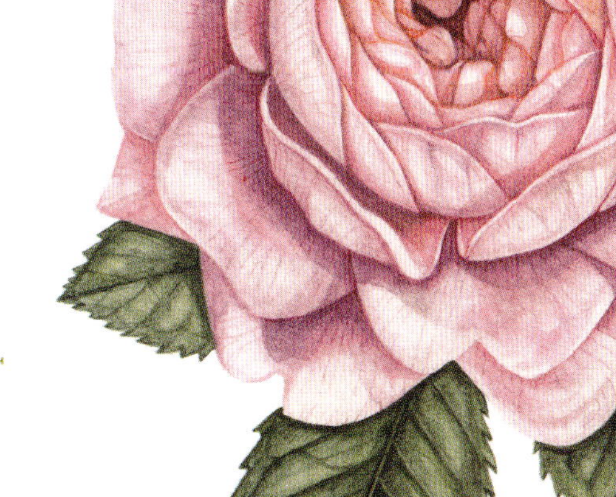

Practice, practice, practice

It is always a good idea to practice new techniques before you begin a painting. Particularly something like the fine lines in step 4. Remember that any mistakes can be patted off with a tissue when wet.

Gallery

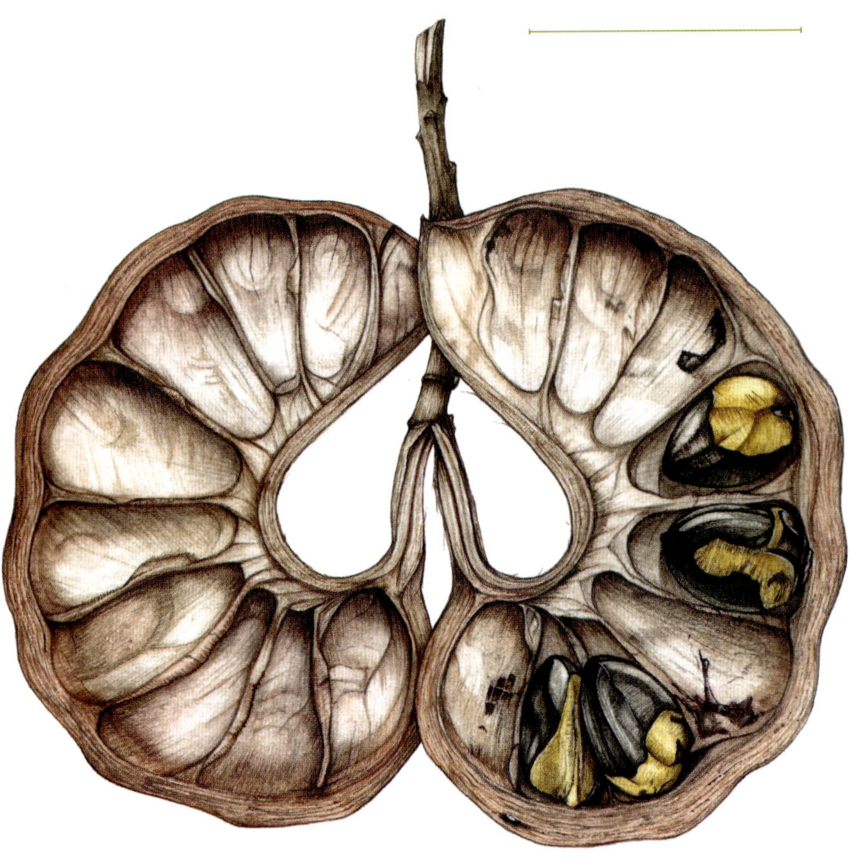

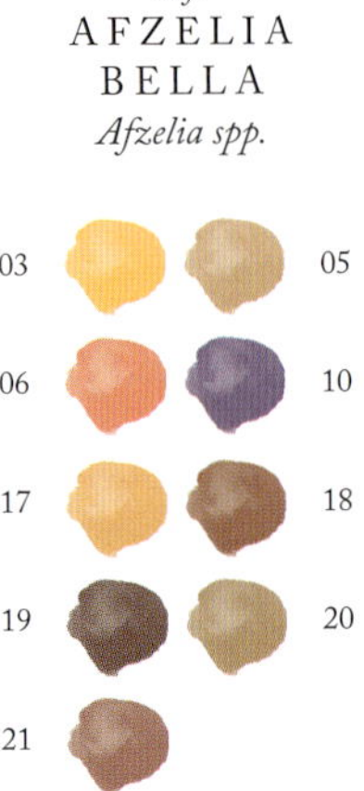

Left
AFZELIA BELLA
Afzelia spp.

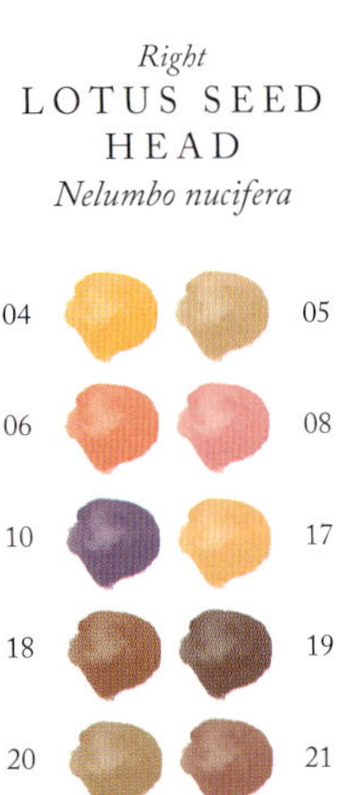

Right
LOTUS SEED HEAD
Nelumbo nucifera

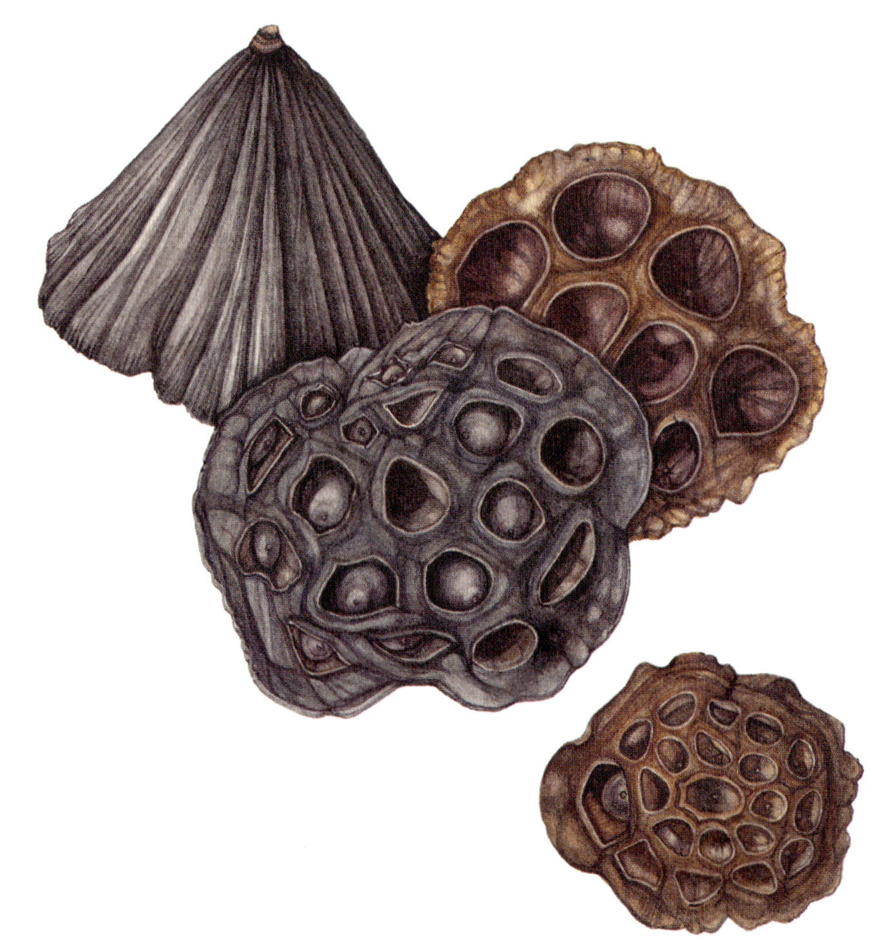

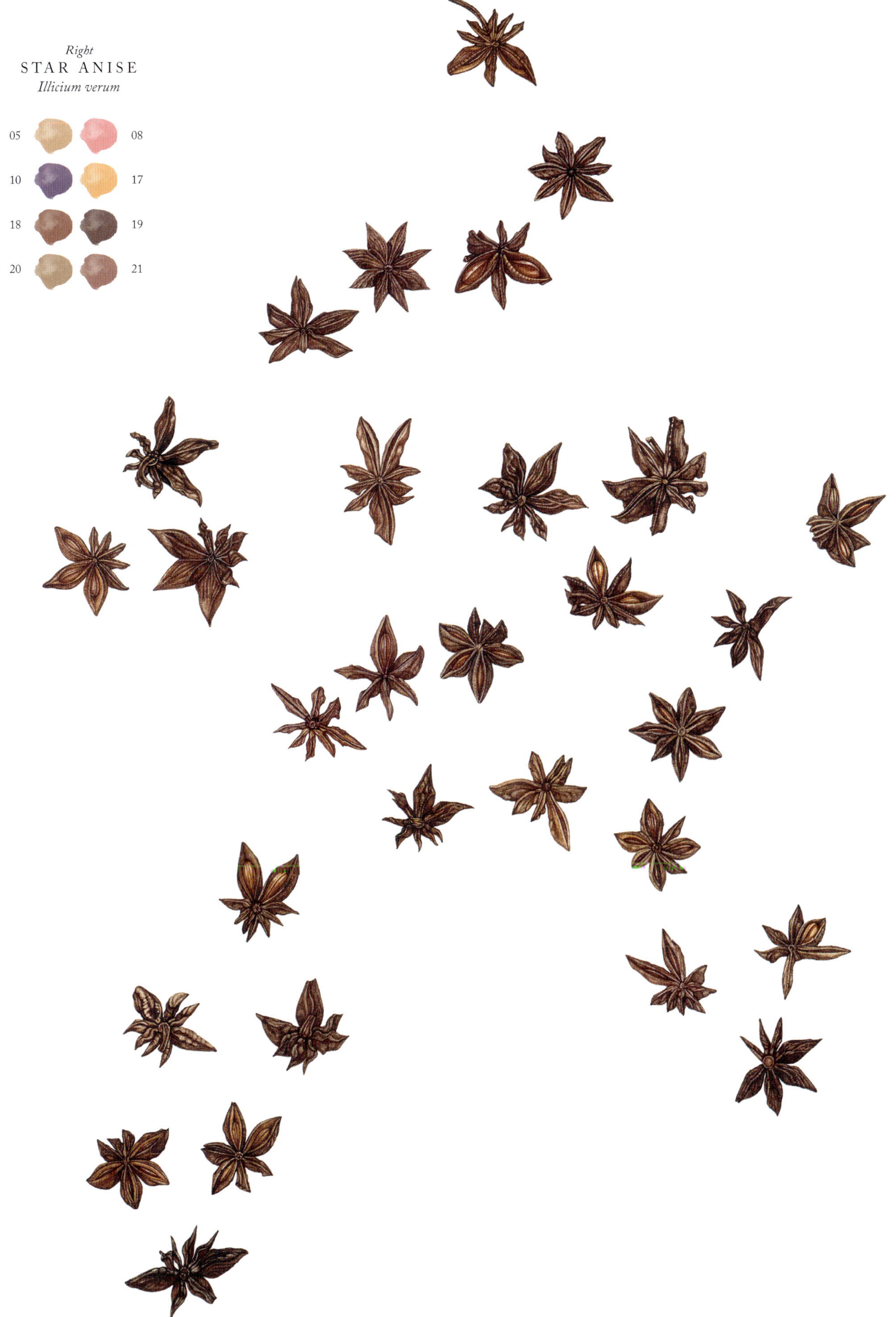

Right
STAR ANISE
Illicium verum

Left
ROSE HIPS
Rosa canina

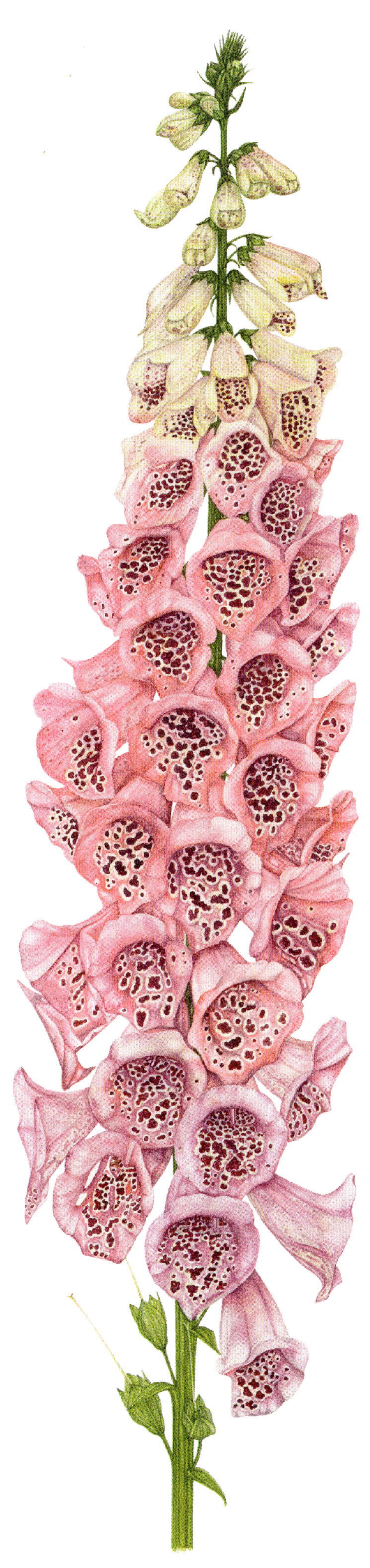

Left
FOXGLOVE
Digitalis purpurea

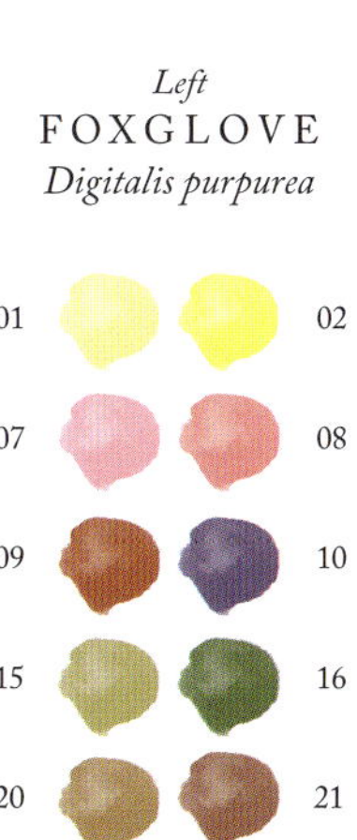

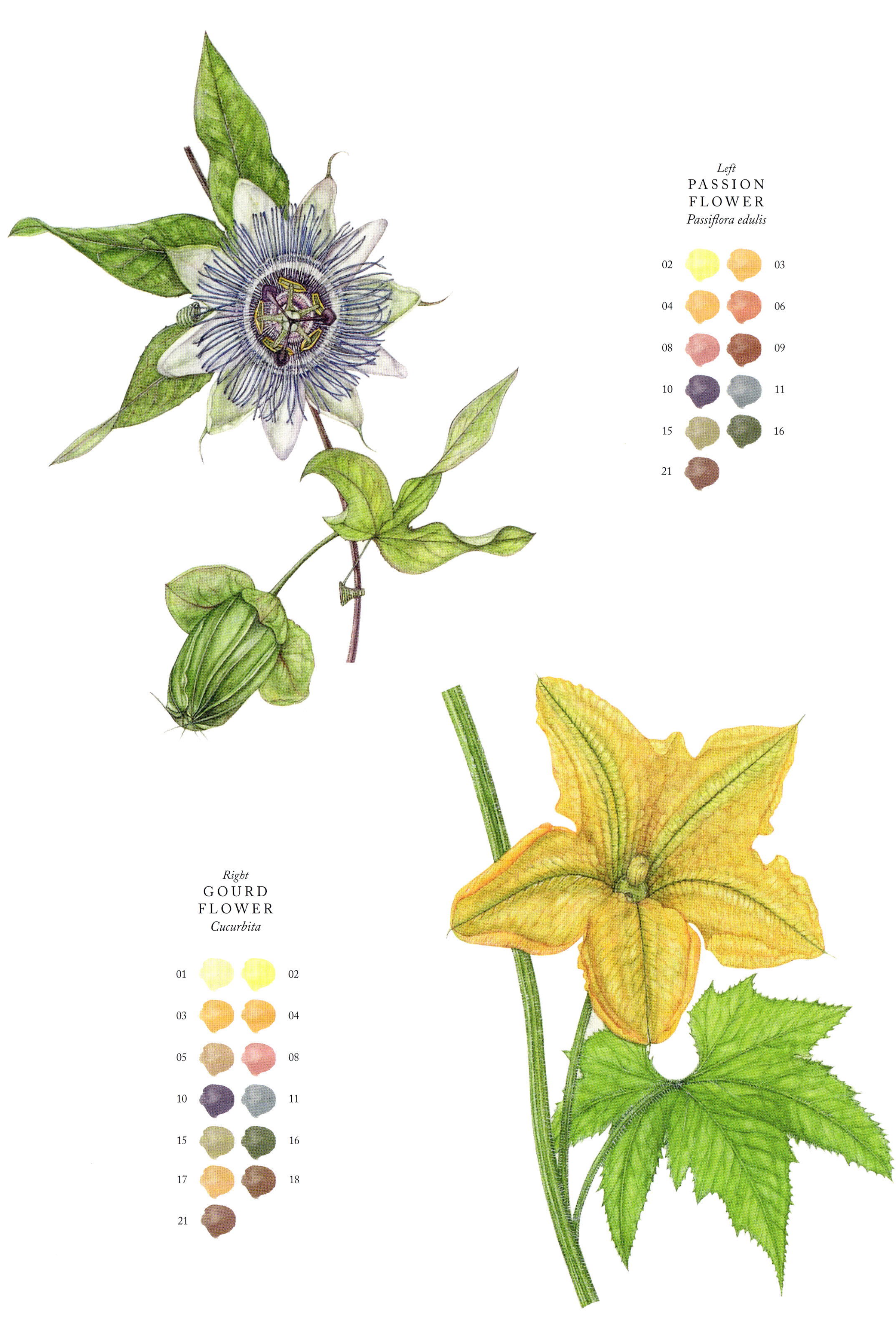

Left
PASSION FLOWER
Passiflora edulis

02 03
04 06
08 09
10 11
15 16
21

Right
GOURD FLOWER
Cucurbita

01 02
03 04
05 08
10 11
15 16
17 18
21

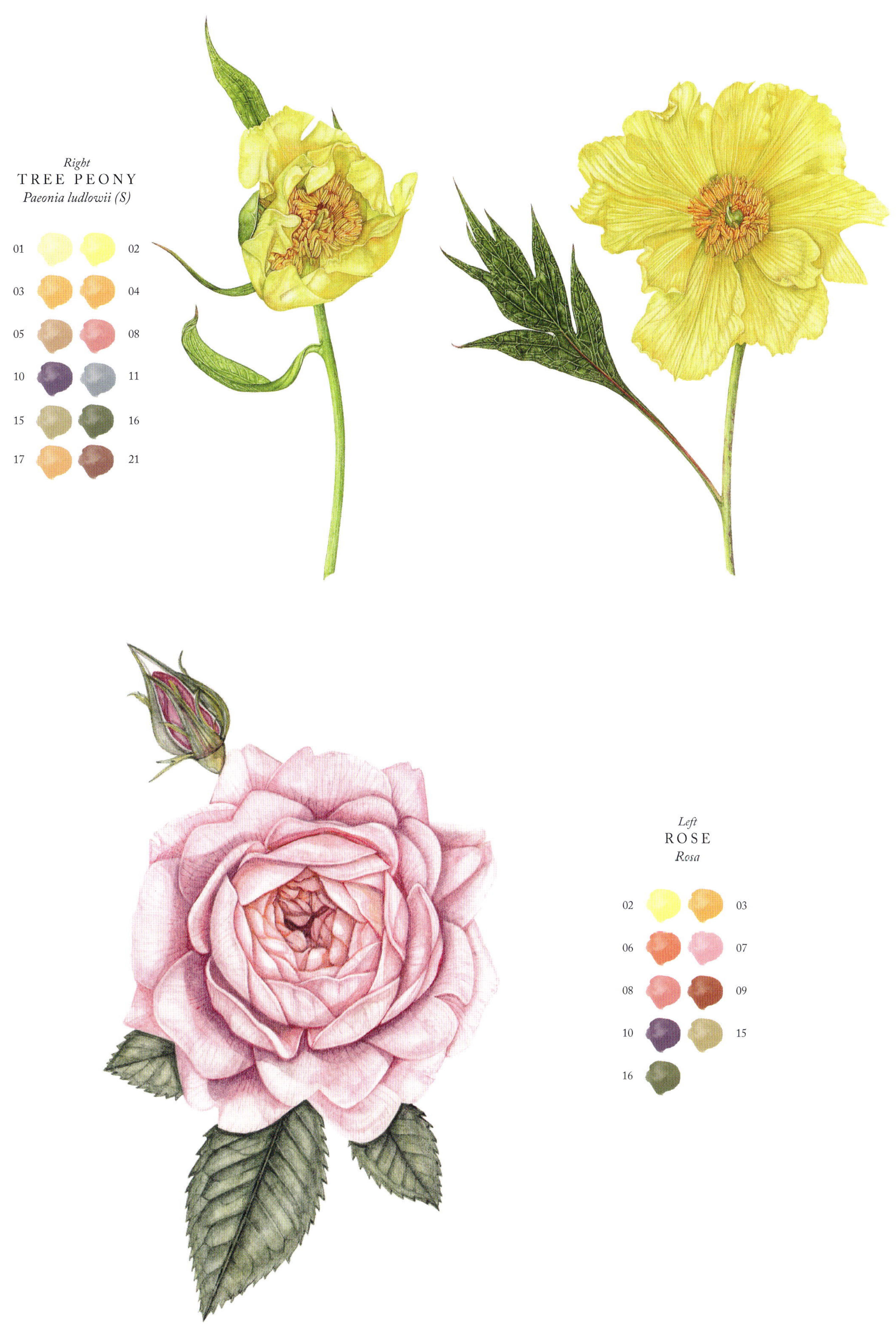

Right
TREE PEONY
Paeonia ludlowii (S)

01 02
03 04
05 08
10 11
15 16
17 21

Left
ROSE
Rosa

02 03
06 07
08 09
10 15
16

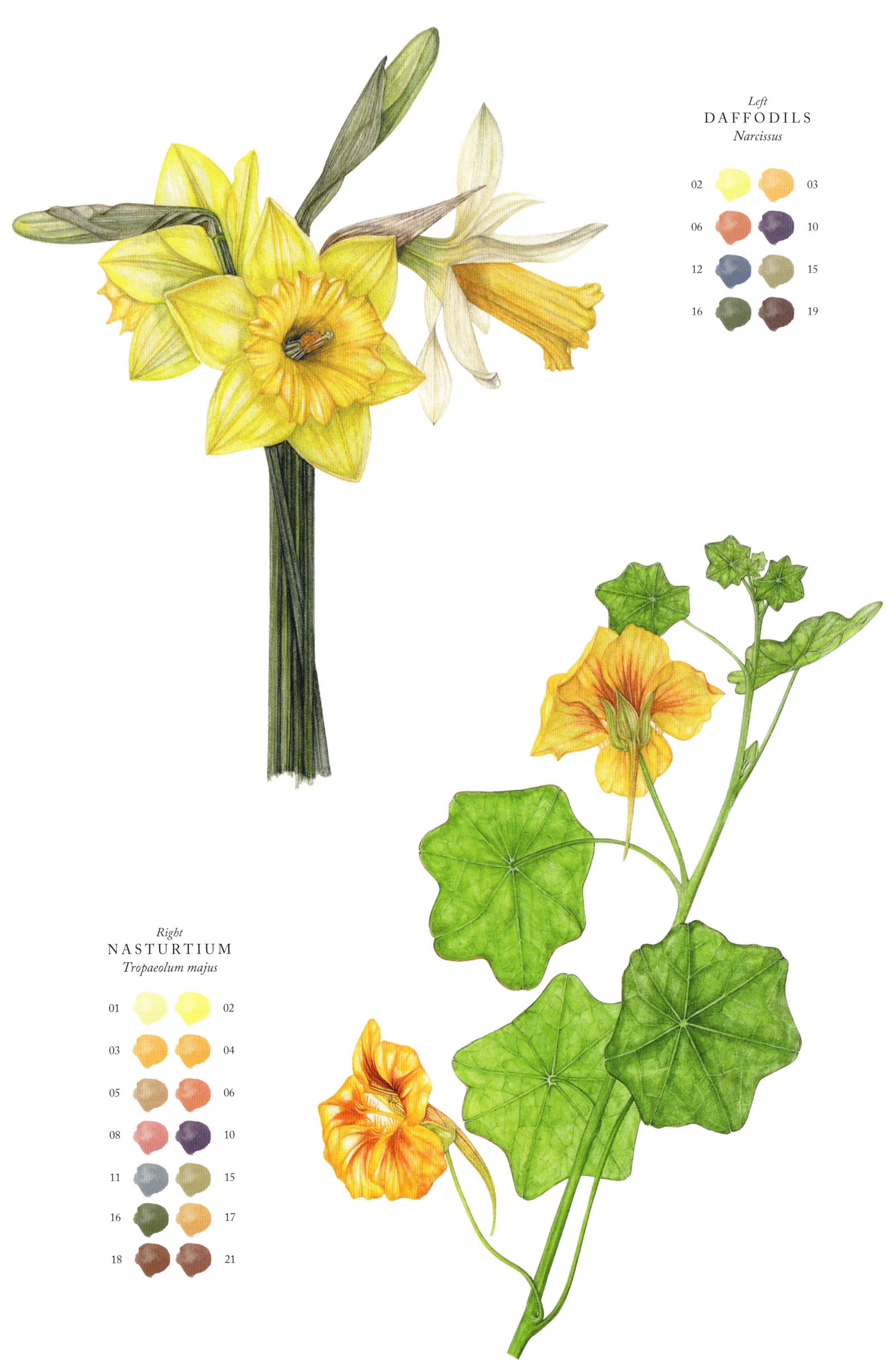

Left
DAFFODILS
Narcissus

02 03
06 10
12 15
16 19

Right
NASTURTIUM
Tropaeolum majus

01 02
03 04
05 06
08 10
11 15
16 17
18 21

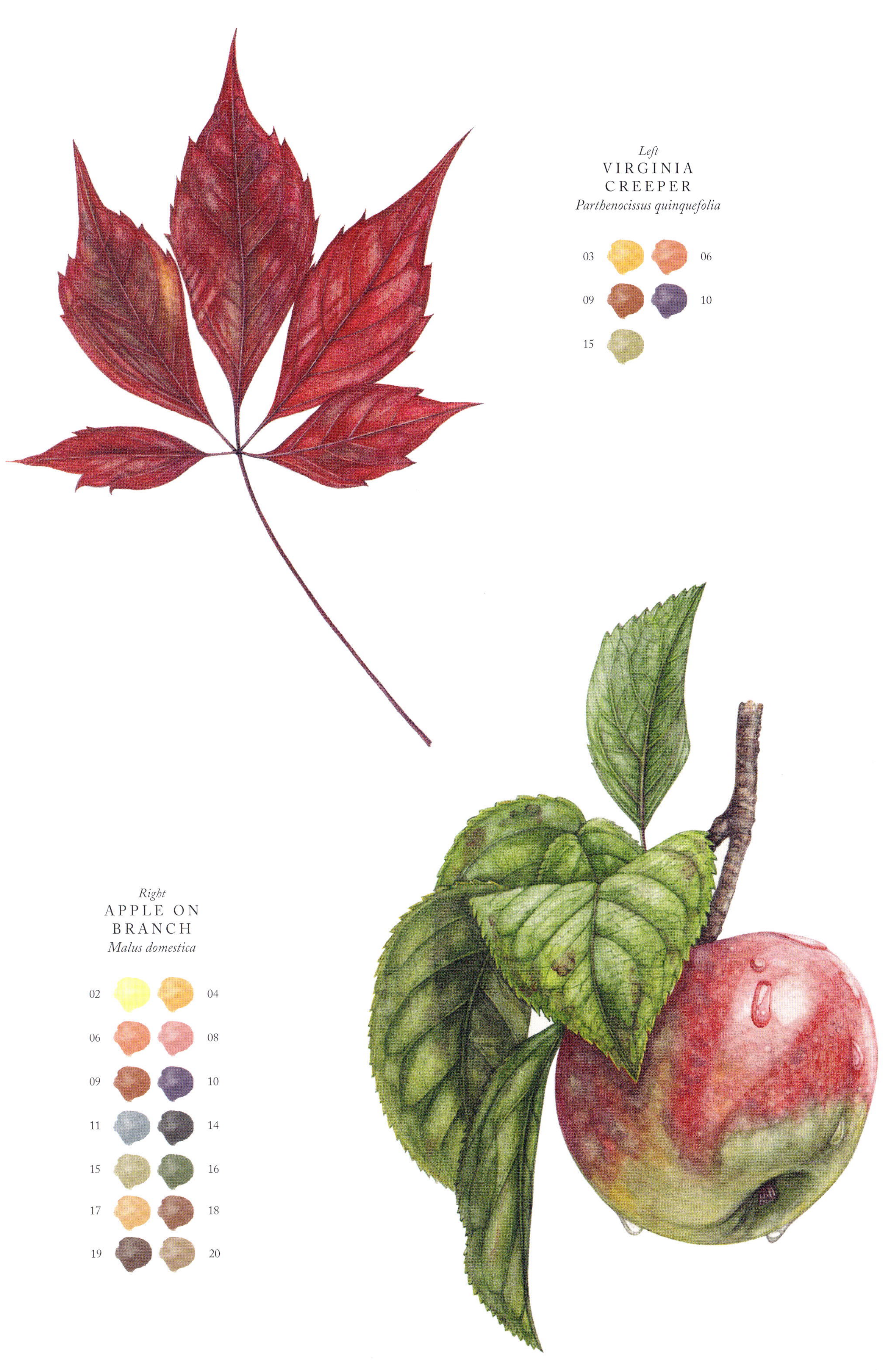

Left
VIRGINIA CREEPER
Parthenocissus quinquefolia

03 06
09 10
15

Right
APPLE ON BRANCH
Malus domestica

02 04
06 08
09 10
11 14
15 16
17 18
19 20

Right
AUBERGINE
Solanum melongena

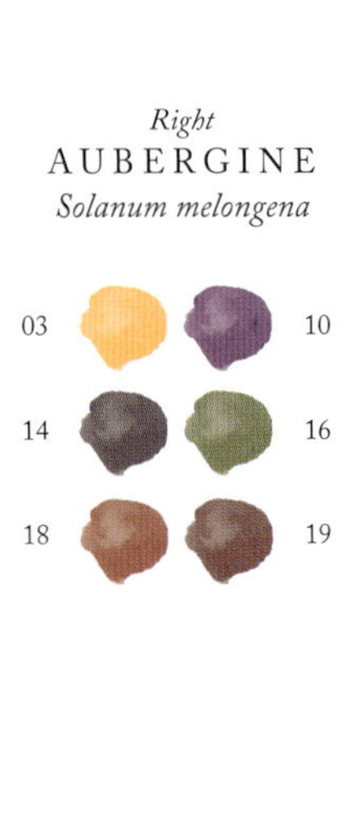

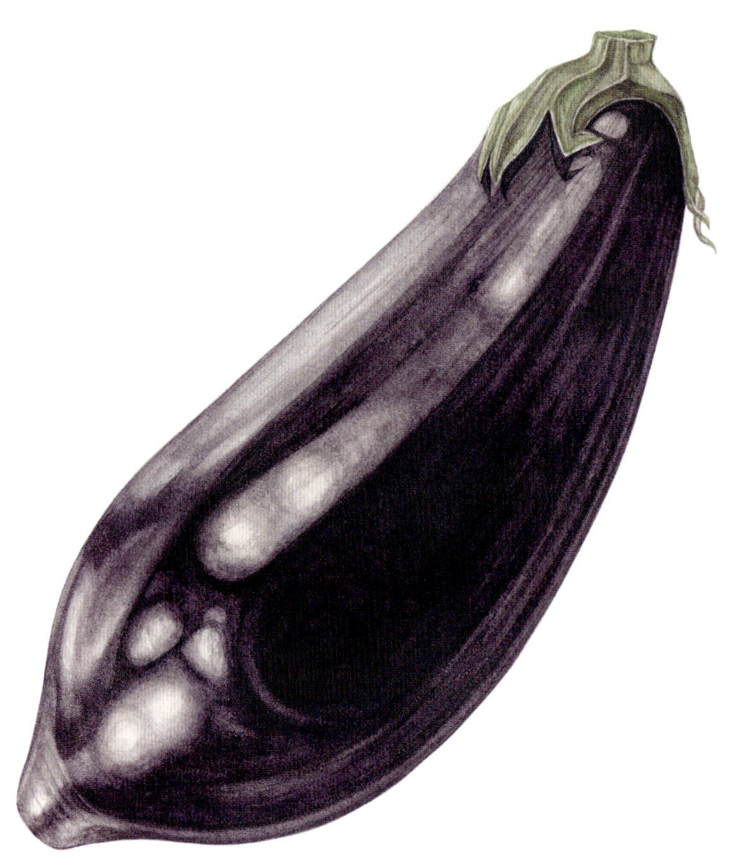

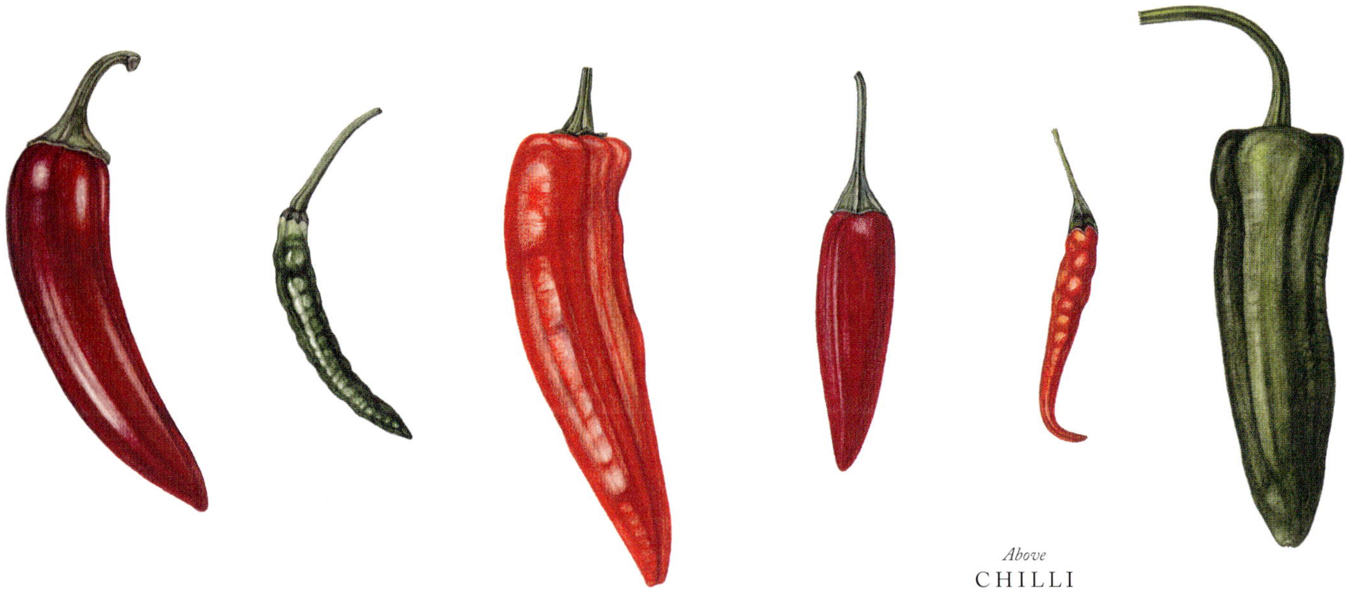

Above
CHILLI
Capsicum annuum

02 06

08 09

10 11

15 16

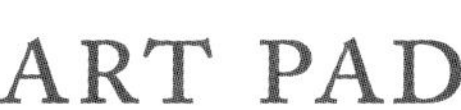

ART PAD

This section contains all the templates you need to complete the paintings in the gallery.

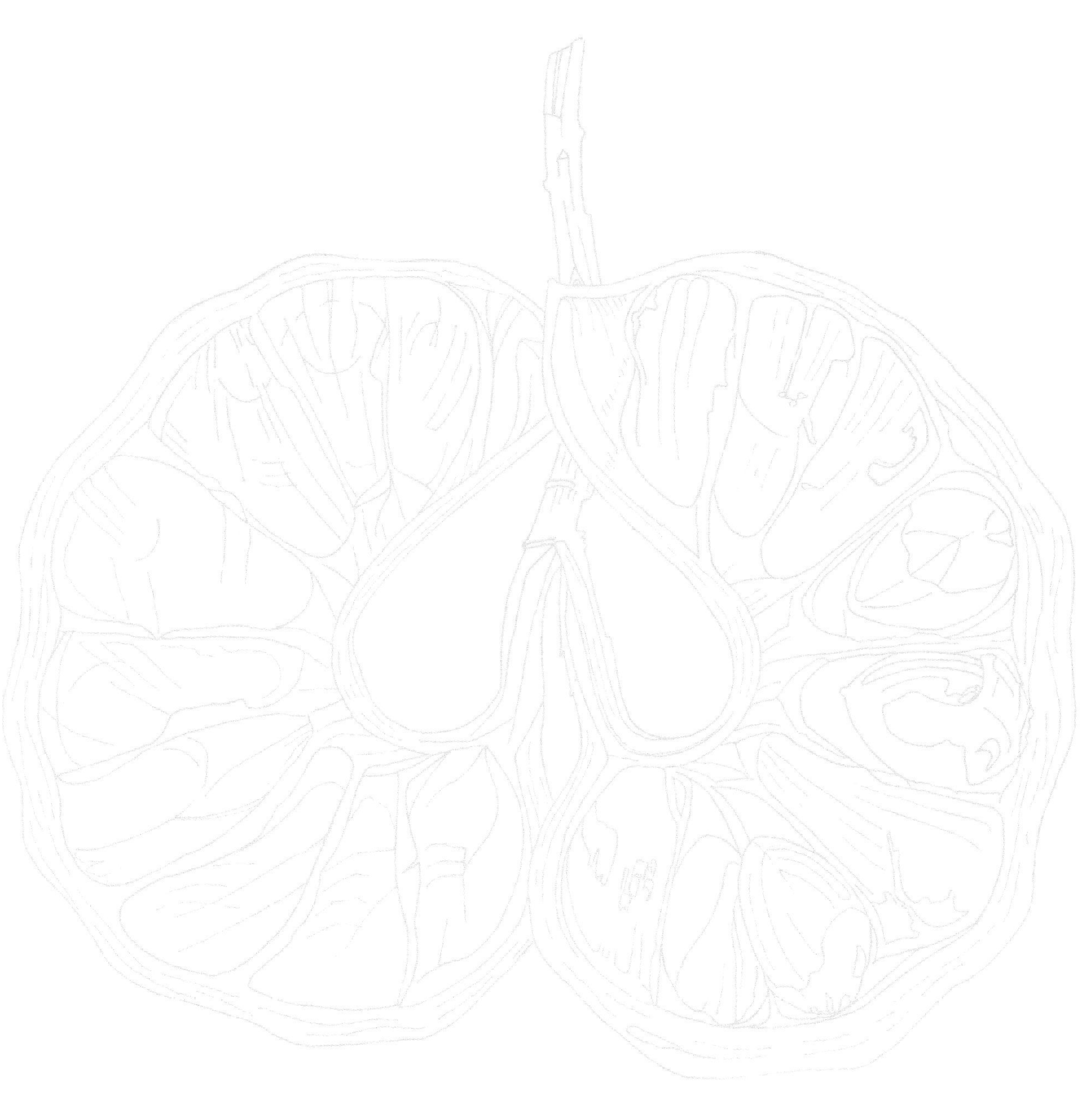

AFZELIA BELLA
Afzelia spp.

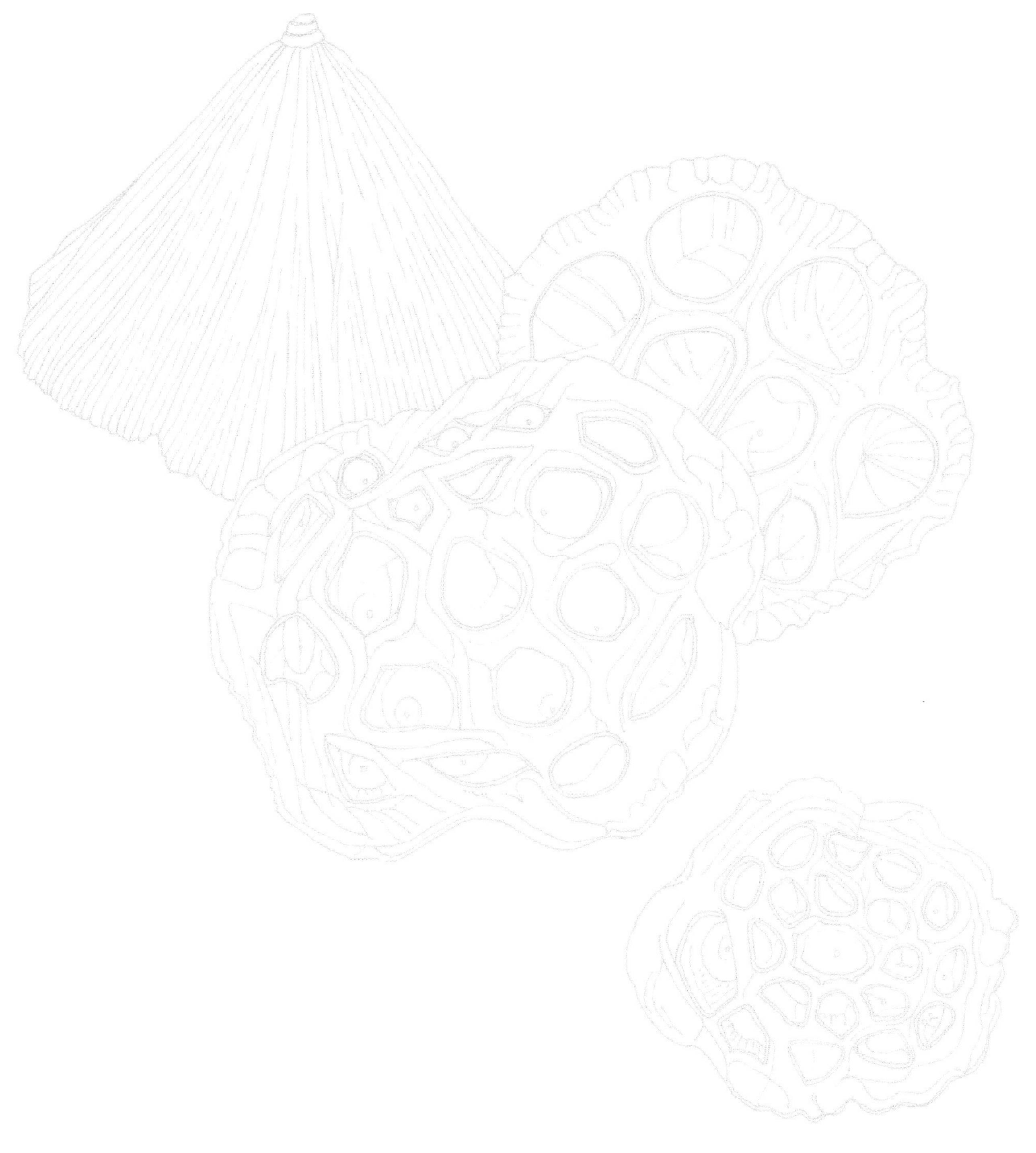

LOTUS SEED HEAD
Nelumbo nucifera

STAR ANISE
Illicium verum

ROSE HIPS
Rosa canina

FOXGLOVE
Digitalis purpurea

PASSION FLOWER

Passiflora edulis

GOURD FLOWER
Cucurbita

TREE PEONY
Paeonia ludlowii (S)

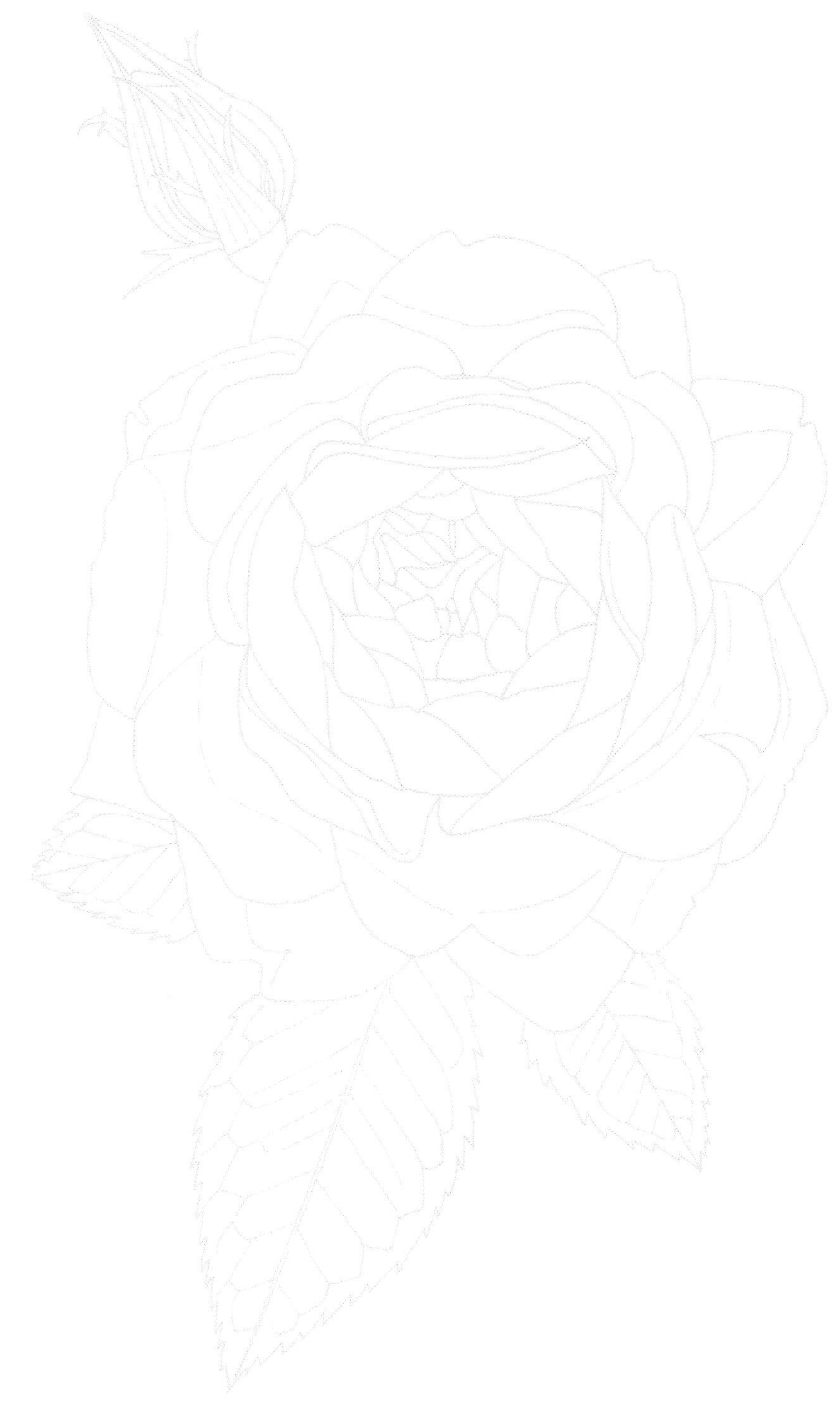

ROSE
Rosa

DAFFODILS
Narcissus

NASTURTIUM
Tropaeolum majus

VIRGINIA CREEPER
Parthenocissus quinquefolia

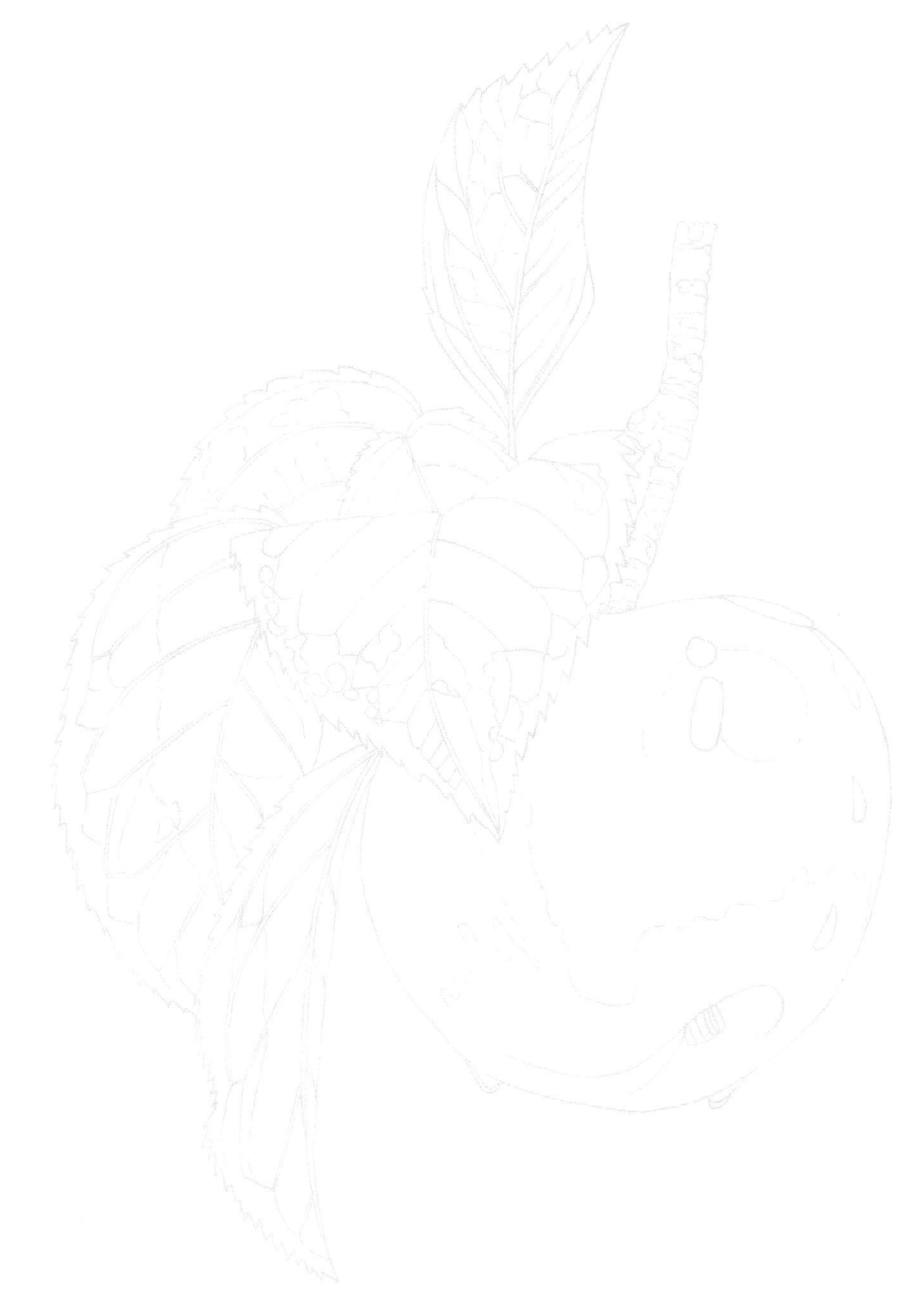

APPLE ON A BRANCH
Malus domestica

AUBERGINE

Solanum melongena

CHILLI

Capsicum annuum